ALCHEMY
ILLUSTRATED

ALCHEMY
ILLUSTRATED
THE QUEST FOR GOLD
& THE ELIXIR OF LIFE

MICHAEL KERRIGAN

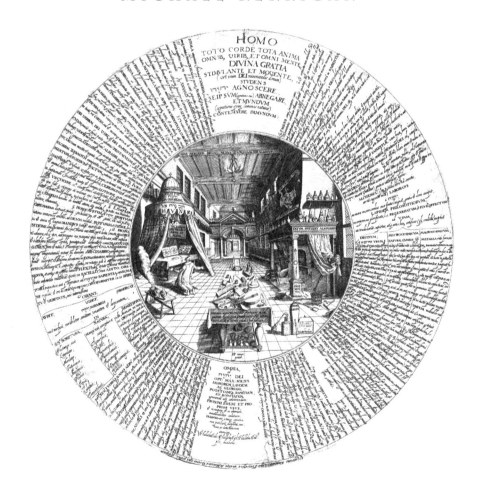

amber
BOOKS

CONTENTS

INTRODUCTION – FOUNTAINS AND FIRST SPRINGS	6
'ALL OBSCURITY SHALL FLY FROM YOU'	56
'ALL IS INTERRELATED'	101
BIBLIOGRAPHY	158
PICTURE CREDITS	160

Introduction:
'Fountains and First Springs'

A serious science? An ancient wisdom? An impressive-sounding nonsense or a flagrant fraud? Alchemy had elements of all these things. Famously, its practitioners set out to find a 'Philosopher's Stone' which would enable them not only to create an elixir of eternal youth but also to transmute base metal into gold. Crazy aims – but they made sense then, and alchemy was arguably as close to being a science as it could have been, methodological rules we take for granted not yet having evolved. A historical survey takes us on a tour of the best and worst of human nature, introducing a riotous assembly of geniuses, charlatans, plodders, dupes and downright rogues.

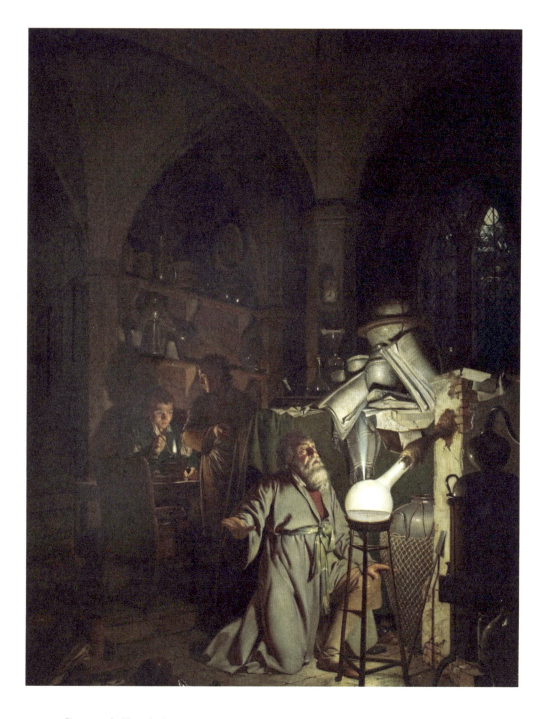

Germany's Hennig Brand discovered phosphorus during an alchemical experiment of 1669. Joseph Wright of Derby captured the moment in *The Alchemist in Search of the Philosopher's Stone* (1771).

Among these last – admittedly fictional – would be Subtle, the appropriately named protagonist of *The Alchemist* (1610). In this dazzling but super-cynical comedy, Ben Jonson (1572–1637) portrays alchemy as essentially fraudulent: 'a pretty kind of game/Somwhat like tricks o'the cards, to cheat a man/with charming.' The 'mark' for Subtle's stratagem, Sir Epicure Mammon, is so unappealing it's a positive pleasure to see him swindled, a boorish blend of stupidity and greed. Just a generation later, though, Isaac Newton (1642–1727) was to be born. Not only was he a real person: he was an indisputably distinguished personage, whose scientific credentials have never been surpassed. A universal law of gravitation was only the most celebrated of his achievements alongside foundational work in everything from electricity to optics, from mechanics to mathematics. But he was an eager student of alchemy, too, taking it every bit as seriously as he did the more conventionally 'scientific' work for which he's remembered now.

The toughest challenge for any history of alchemy is encompassing the contradictions this trinity of characters represent. They overlap and part company in different ways. Sly and resourceful, Subtle has at least a smattering of Sir Isaac Newton's scientific intellect, but is a match for Sir Epicure Mammon in his lack of scruple. Sir Epicure is so foolish as effectively to be devoid of guile; unfortunately, he's devoid of conscience too. Newton's stature is so immense he almost legitimizes the discipline of alchemy all by himself – but the others' folly and dishonesty aren't so easily dismissed. Nor do the difficulties end there. When we bring the more truly high-minded strand in alchemical research more firmly into focus we find ourselves flummoxed by the limitations of early (and even early-modern) 'scientific' thought.

The stunning frontispiece to Stefan Michelspecher's *Cabbala: Mirror of Art and Nature* **(1615) shows how closely alchemy, science, philosophy and theology went hand in hand.**

Ben Jonson's Subtle pulls the wool over another credulous client's eyes in an illustration to his satirical drama, *The Alchemist* (1610).

Substance and Soul

The stated aim of the alchemists was to refine and rarefy the crude physicality of tangible reality so completely as to obtain an essence that left materiality behind. Stephanus of Alexandria (c. 580–c. 640) summed it up well in the seventh century CE. 'It is', he said, 'necessary to deprive matter of its qualities in order to draw out its soul. Copper', he continued, 'is like a man; it has a soul and a body', of which, of course, 'the soul is the most subtile part. The body is the ponderable, material, terrestrial thing, endowed with a shadow.' But, he stressed, under the right conditions, that physical substance could be processed into a 'purer' state.

The different metals, for the alchemists, were just more or less refined versions of the same substance, 'Earth'. In its highest still-physical form this substance became gold, by general consent the highest of the metals. Ultimately, though, it aspired to a still higher state in which it transcended the material for the spiritual realm.

The alchemical symbol for air.

Falsifying the Truth

Stephanus is one of the many brilliant researchers who helped build the discipline of alchemy. That he believed what now seem nonsensical things does not make him a fool. From today's scientific perspective, the problem with his theories is not that they're self-evidently stupid – his account of matter is plausible enough as far as it goes. But it's just an assertion, apparently accepted implicitly: it covered the facts so – as far as he and his contemporaries were concerned – had no need of further testing. Why would one question an account that seemed to 'work'? Paradoxically, perhaps, modern scientific method sees 'falsifiability' as key to finding the truth. To have confidence in the justice of a scientific claim, we have to be able to envisage a way in which – in principle, at least – it might be falsified, shown to be untrue. Otherwise we're just playing games with words.

The idea of falsifiability wasn't explicitly formulated till the twentieth century when it was proposed by the Austrian–British philosopher Karl Popper (1902–94). It was, however, implicit in what we now call 'scientific method' – a rigorous process of coming up with hypotheses, testing (and potentially disproving) them then trying to repeat our tests to check we come up with the same findings. This took shape by gradual degrees from the Enlightenment of the seventeenth century on. 'In order to seek truth,' wrote René Descartes (1596–1650), 'it is necessary … to doubt, as far as possible, all things.' Systematic scepticism became a habit of mind for scientists and philosophers who had for centuries trusted to the authority of their ancient predecessors.

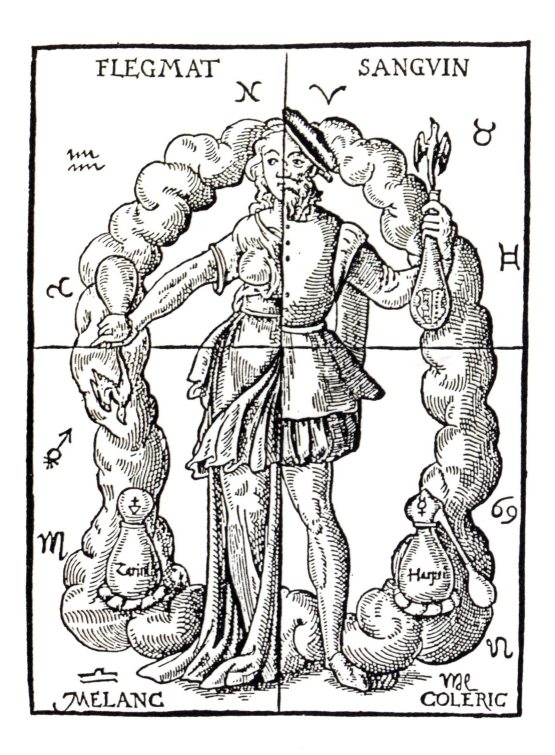

Not only were people's characters seen as conforming overall to certain emotional types or 'temperaments', these different 'humours' were seen as being balanced in different proportions in different individuals.

The descent of a black sun with a sulky face behind a damp horizon represents the state of putrefaction in this illustration from Salomon Trismosin's *Splendor Solis* (c. 1580).

Enduring Influences

But only very slowly. It is startling to find just how recently the ancient ideas still governed scientific thought. The idea that human health was governed by the balance of four 'humours' is believed to have been proposed by the Greek thinker Hippocrates (*c*. 460–*c*. 370 BCE). He claimed that health and mood alike were determined by the balance in the individual of (melancholy) black bile, (choleric) yellow bile, (quiet and passive) phlegm and (upbeat) blood. Galen (129–*c*. 216 CE), who laid the foundations of medieval medicine, did so on the foundations that Hippocrates had built.

The theory's hold was weakened by the boom in anatomical enquiry the Renaissance brought from the fifteenth century then further by the discovery of the circulation of the blood by William Harvey (1578–1657). Harvey's approach helped open the way to a new vision of the body as a sort of organic engine. He himself questioned the role of the humours in controlling the emotions, but their function in physical health would be widely accepted well into the nineteenth century.

Along with the aura of authority that had grown up around these ancient assumptions, a basic inertia ensured that they continued to hold sway. It certainly took something seriously compelling in the way of new research to see what had seemed 'proven' assumptions finally displaced. Florence Nightingale (1820–1910), who pioneered the practice of modern nursing in the 1850s, shared the view of medieval medics that illness was caused by 'miasmas' (contagious clouds of noxious air). Again, it appeared to cover the known facts. 'Germ Theory' wouldn't be firmly established till the 1890s, by which time the internal combustion engine was old news and the Wright Brothers' first flight (1903) just a few years off.

Observational Eccentricities

The theory of 'spontaneous generation' – the view that living things sprang fully formed from inert matter – was almost as enduring. The ancient view that frogs emerged spontaneously from damp mud made observational sense of sorts. But observation isn't infallible. Rightly revered as the Father of Empiricism, Greek philosopher Aristotle (384–22 BCE) had got some way into the formulation of a comprehensive theory of sexual reproduction but still felt drawn irresistibly to the conclusion that insects sprang spontaneously from the soil and maggots from dead meat. It's still startling to find the seventeenth-century Belgian naturalist Jan Baptist van Helmont (1580–1644) proposing that mice could be be brought to life spontaneously from a scattering of grain left wrapped in a grubby rag in a quiet corner. Slowly, inexorably, the evidence against the theory of 'spontaneous generation' accumulated, but it was only finally disproven by the experiments of Louis Pasteur (1822–95) in 1863.

Inherited Assumptions

'Man is dumb; he knows nothing,' says a Sumerian prayer from around 3500 BCE. In humbler moments, modern scientists might say the same. The very notion of a body of knowledge implies the existence of another, of what isn't known, potentially all but infinite in its scale. Modern researchers wouldn't dream of filling the gaps in their understanding with 'wisdom' drawn from mythological tradition or ancient writings whose imagined authority derives only from their age. But this scepticism, as we've seen, has been hard-won. It seemed only natural to earlier civilizations, daunted by the vast incomprehensibility of the universe, to find support in belief systems they'd inherited from their forebears.

Alchemical researchers took their science's obscurity as confirmation of its truth. The peasants holding up a red robe here while Mercury rests on water below come from an eighteenth-century tome.

Jan Baptist van Helmont's work points up both the value of empirical science and the risks of mistakes where understanding was not complete.

The idea that science might be a 'method', an approach to understanding, was utterly alien to cultures who took it to be an established order, an assemblage of known facts. From a twenty-first-century perspective, it is all too easy to appreciate the extent to which this knowledge encompassed several sorts of what we now see as religious or even magical thinking.

But also, conversely, to see that incomprehensibility as a source of wonder. Even in the Palaeolithic people sensed that what they saw wasn't quite the sum of the way things were. Typically, the earliest communities seem to have found religious significance in either their environment, its animals and topographical features (animism) or in their departed ancestors, as communicated with by a priest or shaman. Both traditions brought with them the strong sense of a dimension beyond what was immediately discernible at hand.

The bison and wild cattle depicted in the magnificent cave-paintings of Altamira, Spain, and Lascaux, in southern France, surely had a symbolic significance as well as a representational one. Hunter-gatherer peoples studied in more recent times have endowed key animal species with 'totemic' status, looking to them for a spiritual protection that transcends their importance as a food-source or a threat. Non-figurative designs created 18,000 years ago at La Madeleine, France, and in caves in Cantabria, Spain, appear to confirm conclusively that the earliest humans were accustomed to thinking at a symbolic level; imagining a tier of existence that extended beyond their own.

Magical Thinking

More established civilizations fixed on settled pantheons of gods. Frequently, though, their remits were ill-defined. This was necessary to accommodate the vast unknowability of the spiritual dimension and the universe over which they were supposed to wield control. The Egyptians, for instance, attached enormous importance to something that they called *Heka*, for which the nearest equivalent we have is 'magic'. *Heka* was for imaginative convenience sometimes personified as a god, but more frequently regarded as a pervasive force. 'Magic', writes the Egyptologist Joyce Tyldesley, 'was, at all levels of society, a real and potent power that could be used to protect the innocent and ward off harm.' It was a first aid kit: 'Physicians healed with medical prescriptions supplemented by tried and tested incantations.' It was an arsenal of weapons: 'Kings eliminated remote enemies by burning or smashing their names in temple rituals.' Likely as not their targets would respond in kind. 'Execration texts', calling down all manner of misfortune on those held to have wronged the issuers, have been found at Thebes, Saqqara and other sites in Egypt.

'Let us go to seek the nature of the four elements,' reads the message streaming from this alchemist's vase. Edith Annie Ibbs painted this watercolour in the 1900s.

What appears to be the figure of the Egyptian Physician Hesy-Ra, as shown in his tomb, c. 2660 BCE. Egyptian 'medicine' sounds more like magic to us now.

To this day we tend to think of magic in this same way, as a special power, a practice: the spell of the witch who turned the handsome prince into a frog. But magic has for the most part been more interesting – and ultimately more powerful – as a body of knowledge. For the Egyptians, indeed, it was a way of approaching existence. It encompassed everything: not just rituals (*seshaw*) but medicinal treatments (*pekhret*) and even what we would regard as religious writings (*rw*). 'It could not be separated in any meaningful way from formal religion,' writes Tyldesley; 'nor could it be separated from science.' This sentence is worth pondering, because in the modern age the scrupulous separation of these different domains has been pretty much the cornerstone of serious intellectual enquiry.

Trial and Technology

Today, technology is generally seen as secondary to science, the practical application of ideas thrashed out in theory. In ancient times, however, in the absence of more rigorous ways of thinking, technology had largely to make its own way in the world. In fact, it was on firmer ground, given that innovations could be prompted by chance discoveries and then developed through a process of trial and error. Our modern word 'experiment' comes from the Latin *experimentum* – 'experience' or 'try'. This kind of experimentation – trying things out to see what would happen – certainly did exist in antiquity, in Roman times and before, even if the need for 'control', for verification, had not yet occurred.

'Science' was arguably first put to work by our hominid ancestors in the use of basic tools and, from about 200,000 years ago, in the harnessing of fire – for warmth and for protection against wild beasts. How far this can truly count is questionable, though. 'Science' literally means 'knowledge' – again from a Latin word, *scientia* – and it seems extremely unlikely that these pre-humans came up with any conscious conceptualization of what they were doing.

Gradually, over millennia, though, they learned to use fire for other things: for hardening wooden points, for instance, and cooking food. Eventually, around 24,000 years ago, judging by finds made at Dolni Vestonice in the Czech Republic, they found a way of firing soft clay forms into ornamental or ritual figures. We can only imagine how exciting it was for these first craftworkers to make what amounted to 'artificial stone'. Ceramic vessels came considerably later, but presumably in time to contain the first beers and wines – believed to have been made at an early stage in the Neolithic Period, which saw an agrarian revolution some time around 10,000 BCE. Yeast was used to make the first bread at this time too. All these developments – the use of fire; making pottery; cooking; the fermentation of grain for brewing and baking and of fruit for making wine – could be seen as involving controlled chemical reactions.

Isis, 'Great Enchantress', was first and foremost the Egyptian mother goddess, but she was also revered for her deep understanding of *heka*, 'magic'.

Over 20,000 years ago our forebears had their own religious beliefs and aesthetic values. This woman's head, carved in mammoth ivory, was found at Dolni Vestonice.

The Miracle of Metal

Soon humans were cooking up other things. The earliest known copper finds in Mesopotamia come from Tepe Gawra, near Mosul in northwest Iraq. They date from around 4000 BCE. Discoveries at Tepe Yahya, Iran, suggest that smelting was taking place there by 3800. The Egyptians are also assumed to have started at around that time too. By about 2000 BCE there was a major copper-smelting centre at Ayn Soukhna, on the Red Sea coast. How the first metalworkers learned to manufacture copper can only be guessed at. Archaeologists suspect that shards of green malachite may have found their way into a pottery kiln by accident and that nuggets of pure metal were found after it had been fired.

The first addition of tin to copper to make bronze we know of took place at Al 'Ubaid, near Ur, in Mesopotamia between about 3500 and 3200 BCE. That bronze was an invention of the Sumerians seems to be confirmed by the fact that their language – unlike others of the era – made a distinction between copper (*urudu*) and bronze (*zabar*). Over the centuries that followed, Sumerian and Egyptian workers extracted lead, antimony and iron. They also made brass by adding zinc to copper. Silver was for centuries rarer than gold. By 2000 BCE, however, Mesopotamian workers had developed the process of 'cupellation'. Silver-bearing galena ('lead glance') was heated in an earthen crucible to temperatures of around 1100° C, causing its silver content to fuse with the surrounding lead. Sustained blasting with air from a bellows caused the lead to oxidize, separating out a small amount of silver.

Glass appears to have been seen as another sort of artificial stone. Its manufacture followed a process analogous to those of metal-smelting. Nitrum, a natural soda, was heated up with sand (containing silica and lime). Glass beads were being made in Egypt by 2500 BCE, in Mesopotamia a century or so later; the earliest known recipe we have is in Sumerian–Babylonian and dates from the seventeenth century. The materials used and processes followed are recognizable to modern glass-makers. Glass in its most basic form was at this time bluish-green, because just about all the sand available contained iron. Iron oxides could be added to bring out this 'natural' colour more strongly. Manufacturers became skilled in incorporating metallic oxides and varying heat levels in their furnaces to change the colour of the glass that they produced. Copper oxides made it green, blue, turquoise or red; cobalt gave a brighter, more vibrant blue; manganese tinged it yellow (or in some cases purple); antimony provided a more opaque yellow or white.

Colour Coded?

Colour was clearly crucial. The jewellery these cultures created shows how fascinated they were by the range they could achieve by alloying metals and working skilfully with glass. Gold alone came in a range of shades, from bright yellow to near-grey and taking in brick red, purple plum-colour and rose-pink. Especially in the early days when metal tools and weapons weren't yet routinely used (the 'Iron Age' wouldn't begin in earnest till the end of the second millennium BCE), the primary appeal of metal technology was the artistic possibilities it opened up, and it seems likely that this marvellous new palette was one of the major attractions.

The figure of Thoth is seen here adorning Ramses III's mortuary temple (c. 1155 BCE), but his reputed wisdom was to inform the lore of alchemy for centuries subsequently.

Made around 2050 BCE, this figure of King Shulgi of Ur is made from smelted copper. He carries a basket of construction materials in token of his importance in building the Sumerian state.

Much remains obscure, of course, and while it may well be that special significances were attached to specific shades, this is all mysterious to us. The Egyptians appear to have prized blue above all other colours, working extensively with lapis lazuli and turquoise. They developed their own synthetic version, combining sand, green malachite, chalk and salt to make a pigment known today as 'Egyptian blue'. Suffice it to say that, by the first millennium BCE, ancient craftworkers had developed an impressive portfolio of pure and alloyed metals, along with a range of glass, ceramics and other 'artificial stones'.

Workers' Rites

We naturally refer to these early craftspeople as 'workers' because that's the only description that makes sense to us in our modern, post-industrial age. It seems unlikely, though, that their contemporaries saw them quite so prosaically: they may even have had a sort of priestly status. Long after it had become routine as a practice, smelting seems to have retained a powerful mystique. Never does it appear to have been just a job. The discovery of what seem to have been sacrificial offerings in the walls of furnaces for both glass-making and metal-smelting suggests that these processes were seen not as humdrum 'work' but as religious rituals. That the offerings were often human embryos suggests that the ancients saw the extraction of pure metal or glass from rough earth ore as a sort of mystic mineral midwifery, enabling Mother Earth to bring forth her treasures to the world.

Analogously, there's some suggestion that Sumerian smiths saw their materials as somehow sexed, darker, harder 'male' minerals to be combined with softer 'female' ones. Overlapping with this gendered paradigm, however, was one which associated dark colours with night and light with day, a view which in its turn linked up to the astrological theories emerging in Mesopotamia at this time. Naturally enough, perhaps, the Babylonians saw associations between gold and the Sun and silver and the Moon, but they went further, finding a kinship between lead and Saturn, electrum and Jupiter, copper and Venus and tin and Mercury. It appears that, in keeping with the air of mysticism surrounding the smelting of metal, it was conducted in coordination with the Zodiac, the signs dictating which were the most propitious times. Different blends were seen as cementing different couplings of the planets for different purposes. The resulting alloys had a symbolic significance as well as a physical function and aesthetic appeal.

The alchemical symbol for gold.

The bottle factory depicted here dates from modern times – the nineteenth century – but the art of glassblowing had been practised since ancient times.

The 'science' underpinning the organization of this fifteenth-century German pharmacy seems utterly unfamiliar now. It wouldn't have done to many ancient scholars.

Stars and Science

Nothing better illustrates the continuity between religion, magic and science in the ancient world than the emergence of astrology in Mesopotamia in the second millennium BCE. All ancient cultures appear to have tracked the journeys of the stars and planets around the heavens, Neolithic communities arranging their monumental sites around the solstices which signalled the symbolic 'death' and 'rebirth' of the Sun each year. The Egyptians made their observations the basis of a carefully constructed calendar, around which they arranged an elaborate ritual programme, geared ultimately to their overriding cult of death. It was in Babylonia, though, that scholars came up with the idea that the movements of the constellations exerted a real influence on the lives of the people living down below. The relative disposition of the constellation Aries and the planet Mars might determine the fortunes of a marriage, a lunar eclipses the outcome of a military expedition.

Astrology can be seen as epitomizing both the strengths and weaknesses of ancient science. Taking off from an admirably firm foundation of accurate observation and on the virtuoso calculations of mathematicians to whom we owe the first beginnings of the discipline of geometry, it made extravagantly far-fetched flights of fancy and called it 'wisdom'.

Divination

'Now may my god open his innermost soul to me with all his heart,' said the prayer of Kantuzili, a Hittite priest (*c.* 1400 BCE). 'May my god either speak to me in a dream ... or let a diviner of the Sun-god speak to me by reading from a liver in extispicy.' The practice of 'extispicy', the examination of an animal's entrails, looking for unusual shapes or markings to find clues to what the future held, was one of several forms of divination which remained popular until Roman times. The way a flock of birds configured itself in flight; the behaviour of a group of ants; the formation in which a handful of pebbles or bone fragments landed when they were thrown ... All these things could be interpreted by a priest with the necessary powers or skills, as could the meaning of an eclipse or of a memorable dream. Divination didn't of course have any direct bearing on the emergence of alchemy, but what we know of it helps open up a window on the ancient mind. The ways it worked; the connections that it made and the meanings it found in what to us seem utterly random events: these help give us some sense of the thinking that underpinned the earliest attempts at science.

Lord Baal was sued to by diviners who hoped he'd help them prophesy the future. Ugarit, Syria, where this figure was found, was one of his most important shrines.

The Kashite King Melishipak presents his daughter to the goddess Nannaya. A star, sun and moon float protectively above. The art of astrology first appeared in Mesopotamia.

Arcane Knowledge

The mystery surrounding the metalworkers' craft encouraged the emergence of a code of secrecy, making them a quasi-masonic brotherhood. 'Let him that knoweth show him that knoweth,' warns a glassmaking text from the seventeenth century BCE: 'but he that knoweth shall not show him that knoweth not!' The metalworker was no mere labourer but the initiate of a secret company with privileged access to a wealth of occult knowledge. (To a literal wealth as well, of course: the secrecy of the occupation had the additional benefit of closing it off to outsiders, and the competition they would bring.)

Part magical, part religious: this mystique around metallurgy and glass-making occupied the intellectual space in which we might have expected scientific theory to operate. Egypt's mortuary cult helped make sense of the work by giving it a ritual context, while in Mesopotamia astrology did the same. Neither of these visions made even the slightest attempt to explain *why* this lump of rock, heated up, yielded globules of gold; another one a seepage of silver or a trickle of tin. Not until the first millennium BCE did anything approaching such a theory start to emerge. It did so under the aegis of the Greeks. Perhaps – though we can only speculate – because their democratic systems of government placed more of a premium on individual enquiry and questioning than could be admitted in the authoritarian monarchies around which earlier civilizations had been built.

First Steps Towards Science

It is to Thales of Miletus (*c*. 625–*c*. 545 BCE) that the inauguration of 'natural philosophy' has traditionally been credited. Before he came along, the Greeks, like the Mesopotamians and Egyptians, had been content to explain the phenomena of Nature by reference to an array of inherited myths and what we would now call 'folk beliefs'. Thales tried to explain the world, using 'deductive' reasoning to draw inferences for specific cases from what he saw as general laws. Hence, his application of principles he'd established through his astronomical studies to predict a solar eclipse in 585 BCE. And, it's said, to have calculated the height of Egypt's pyramids by comparing the shadow they cast with those of a stick.

As we've seen, though, empirical observation may mislead. Thales' over the years led him to the conclusion that, ultimately, at the deepest level, everything was some form or other of Water. Again, as far as it went, this account covered the facts of existence as they appeared. But then so did the explanation of Anaximenes of Miletus (*c*. 585–25) that all matter was derived from Air, which took on denser and more solid states through 'condensation' or lighter ones by 'rarefaction'.

Elemental Origins

A century later, Empedocles (*c*. 494–*c*. 434 BCE) proposed that the elements were fourfold: Earth, Water, Air and Fire, eternally bound by love and held apart by the force of strife. Moisture and heat were differentiating factors: Earth was cold and dry while Water was cold and (obviously) damp; Air hot and damp while Fire was hot and dry. Hippocrates, we've seen, argued that these relations were re-created within the human body, in which a balance of warmth and cold, moisture and dryness was needed to maintain health.

The value of extispicy – the 'reading' of animal entrails – seemed self-evident for centuries. This Old Babylonian clay model of a sheep's liver was made around 1800 BCE.

Reputedly the work of the great French medieval alchemist Nicolas Flamel (c. 1330–1418), 'The Fair on the Mountain' shows alchemical processes in allegorical form.

Thanks to the plurality and dynamism it encompassed, Empedocles' theory rang true in a way its predecessors hadn't: it would remain the consensus for a millennium and a half. This despite early criticism from Theophrastus (*c.* 371–*c.* 287 BCE), who questioned whether fire could truly be an element if it depended on the consumption of other materials for its continuing existence. Dissenting voices of this sort meant that Greek science did allow for theories to be challenged. It wasn't built into the system, though, and such challenges were – like Theophrastus' – easily ignored. Broadly-speaking, we can see how all these theories anticipate Stephanus' views that what we now see as different elements were more or less refined versions of the same few basic things. This sense of a sliding scale of purity struck a chord with a people accustomed to the mythohistory established by the poet Hesiod (*c.* 700 BCE) of humanity's decline from an idyllic 'Golden Age', through ages of Silver and Bronze, to a wretched one of Iron.

Real vs Ideal

In one sense, the classical Greek thinkers of the fourth century let a light of understanding come flooding into human existence, but even Aristotle, we've seen, could get things wrong. In any case, empiricism wasn't the only philosophical game in town: Plato (*c.* 425–348) came close to contradicting it with his argument that material things were just the imperfect bodying-forth of ideal 'forms', the reality we perceived no more than a veil behind which a more spiritual truth was concealed. This idea fostered the same sort of occultist thinking as had grown up around the metalworking trade in earlier times. Enlightenment might be generally desirable but it wasn't to be generally available: it was inherently secret, the property of a small elite.

Cultural Conquests

In 336, Alexander III (356–23) became King of Macedon, a relatively poor and backward state in the north of Greece. Not that the states to the south were anything like as rich or progressive as they had been a century or so before, when Athens had enjoyed its 'Golden Age'. Alexander was immensely ambitious, though. Intellectually, as befitted one who as a young princeling had been given Aristotle as his tutor, but even more so in his hunger for military renown. No sooner had he ascended his throne than he left it, embarking on one of the most glorious campaigns of conquest the world has ever seen. Asia Minor (modern Turkey), the Middle East and Egypt were all under the control of the Persian Empire at this time. In 333, Alexander defeated Darius III at Issus and two years after that he triumphed at Gaugamela, securing an empire that stretched all the way from Greece to northwest India. He founded cities wherever he went, naming several of them 'Alexandria' after himself.

Alexander's reign was finally to be as brief as it had been glorious. In 323, in Babylon, he fell ill and died. The world's greatest empire immediately became the world's greatest power vacuum. Alexander's generals, backed by their armies, fell to fighting over who should succeed. The war raged on for years, passing on to the generation below as the elder generals were joined by their sons. Finally, three separate realms were left. Egypt fell to Alexander's great friend Ptolemy (*c.* 367–282 BCE); Seleucus (*c.* 358–281 BCE) reigned in Persia and northwest India, while Antigonus (382–01 BCE) took Greece and western Asia.

Thales of Miletus is portrayed by Jacob de Gheyn, more than a millennium after his death. But his thought remained more or less current in the seventeenth century.

The Greek philosopher Empedocles cranes upwards from a window to watch the skies in a painting by the Italian artist Luca Signorelli (1502).

This left much of the known world under Macedonian rule. 'Can you suppose,' asked the Athenian statesman Demetrius of Phaleron (Polybius, *Histories*, 29, 21), 'if some god had warned … that in fifty years the very name of the Persians, who once were masters of the world, would have been lost, and that the Macedonians, whose name was before scarcely known, would have become masters of it all, that they would have believed it?' Just as up-and-coming Rome would be in the century or so that followed, though, Macedonia was culturally conquered by its conquest, Greece. The three new kingdoms shared what has been called a 'Hellenistic' culture (from *Hellas*, the Greeks' own name for their country).

A Hybrid Hellenism

But this description is itself misleading, concealing as it does the extent to which in practice Hellenism was a hybrid culture, absorbing influences from the peoples it had subjugated in Persia, Mesopotamia, Anatolia, Syria and Egypt. The creation of so wide a trading area under Greek rule allowed a cultural commerce too. The succession of wars between the Ptolemaic, the Seleucid and the Antagonid kingdoms only served to further this creative fusion of East and West.

Three continents and several civilizations met at Alexandria, the great seaport the conqueror had founded in 331 BCE at the mouth of the Nile Delta. This part of Egypt had been under Persian occupation at the time he took it. Boats brought cotton, grain and luxury goods from up and down the Nile Valley, while seagoing vessels plied back and forth across the eastern Mediterranean. To Greece, of course, but also to the coasts of Asia Minor (modern Turkey), Syria and Lebanon where they linked up with the overland camel caravans. A famous lighthouse, the Pharos, supposedly standing 100 m (330 ft) tall, guided traffic in and out of Alexandria's harbour.

A Hub of Learning

The Great Library of Alexandria would be a beacon of a different sort, a source of enlightenment for the wider world. Tradition has it that Ptolemy I placed Demetrius of Phaleron – now in exile here after political difficulties in Athens – in charge of collecting books. The structure to house them wasn't built till the reign of his son Ptolemy II (309–246 BCE). The library grew and grew through the Ptolemaic reigns that followed, finally holding up to half a million scrolls.

Ptolemy's original ambition appears to have been to underline the new Egypt's 'Greekness' by showcasing editions of Homer (*c.* eighth century), and the great Athenian dramatists (Aeschylus (*c.* 525–455 BCE), Sophocles (*c.* 496–405 BCE), Euripides (*c.* 480–406 BCE), Aristophanes (*c.* 446–*c.* 386 BCE) …). Over time, though, the library's scope expanded: antique papyruses from up and down Egypt were acquired – though these were translated into Greek. Contemporary Egyptian priests had to provide Greek editions of their works for the Great Library. Alexandria-based merchants were charged with bringing back books from all the different countries they travelled in or traded with; books found on vessels docked in Alexandria's harbour were impounded.

**Aristotle discourses eloquently to an admirably thoughtful-looking Alexander.
The prince's future conquests would open up a community of learning across the ancient world.**

Seen here (c. 1438) by Luca della Robbia, Plato and Aristotle argue a point as, essentially, they always have done, representing the realist and idealist strains in western thought.

Again, the library authorities had all these books translated into Greek, upholding Ptolemy's original ideal but at the same time opening up a new and much more cosmopolitan version of Greek culture. Eventually, along with unrivalled holdings in Greek and Egyptian writing, the Great Library had texts originating in every language known at the time, including religious works relating the Buddhist, Hindu, Jewish and (Persian) Zoroastrian faiths. Learning followed learning: Alexandria soon became a centre not just of history and philosophy but of medicine and mathematics too.

A Pagan Pluralism

And of theology. 'The idea that one religion is false and another true is essentially Christian,' said the English writer E.M. Forster (1879–1970), exaggerating slightly, 'and had not occurred to the Egyptians and Greeks who were living together at Alexandria.' It's true that, already worshipping a plurality of deities, pagans didn't feel as outraged as adherents of the monotheistic religions would have at the thought of tolerating the different divinities of other creeds. The Ptolemies had held on to their Greek pantheon but were quite comfortable accepting the Egyptian gods and goddesses, even combining them 'syncretically' with their own.

Hence the association they made between Dionysos, Greek god of wine, intoxication and mystic trances, and Osiris, Egyptian god of the afterlife and its unknowns, whom they also merged with Apis, Egypt's sacred bull-god, to make a new deity, Serapis. The cult of Serapis was promoted by the Ptolemaic state as a way of maintaining authority over a fundamentally divided Graeco-Egyptian society. But it also exemplified its openness to ideas and influences from every hand.

A Basis for Building

Under Roman occupation from 30 BCE, Ptolemaic Egypt remained a hub of learning. The science and scholarship of the ancient world were concentrated here. That science was limited in key respects, we've seen, but much had still been learned since deep antiquity and research had steadily sharpened in its focus under the Greeks. If we look to the Alexandria of this time to find the foundation on which modern science was built we're liable to find ourselves illuminated and intrigued but finally dissatisfied. If, however, we seek the basis on which alchemy would build over subsequent centuries, we find that we have everything we need. For one, real experience and expertise in working with metals, glass and ceramics. Second, and as a consequence of this, a wider and more general appreciation of how the admixture of different substances, or the application of heat, might make for transformative change.

Less tangible, but as important, we find a 'scientific' framework which set a premium on purity – and saw it as something that might be achieved in progressive stages. Then, too, we find a powerful sense of reality as profoundly mysterious, often counterintuitive, like the metamorphosis of grubby rock into shining metal, dull, tawny sand into beautiful clear glass. So strange did it find reality, indeed, that it saw its essential truths as being reserved for a very few initiates and only to be discussed in the most oblique of terms. 'Was not all the knowledge/of the Aegyptians writ in mystic symbols?', Ben Jonson's Subtle would ask the gullible Sir Epicure Mammon 1,600 years later:

In a nineteenth-century illustrator's exotic imagination, scholars study in the Great Library of Alexandria, in c. 200 BCE, when it really was a centre of learning for the world.

A syncretic combination of Greek and Egyptian influences, Serapis served to symbolize the authority of an overarching Ptolemaic state. His influence endured – as this Roman statue shows.

Are not the choicest fables of the poets,

That were the fountains and first springs of wisdom

Wrapp'd in perplexed allegories?

He has a point, of course, but it's only too obvious how easy it would be to exploit a discipline which held up its unfathomability as its guarantee of truth.

Purportedly by the Persian Prophet Zoroaster (c. 600 BCE), the Clavis Artis ('Key of Art') dates from the sixteenth century CE. Here a half-reptilean female figure consorts with the sun, the moon and stars.

'All Obscurity Shall Fly from You'

The Birth of Christ ushered in the so-called 'Common Era', but only assumed its historiographical importance in retrospect. The Christians were to begin with just one of many minor Jewish sects. Even after its expansion amongst the gentiles, their Church would have little political or cultural clout until Constantine I (c. 272–337) was converted in 312. Christianity would become the official Church of the Roman Empire in 380. That empire was divided by then, its Western section severely weakened, but it still extended from Spain to Syria, from the Scottish Borders to the Valley of the Nile.

**The sense of scholarly continuity was important to the alchemists.
Here ancient sages look down proprietorially on seventeenth-century workers.
From Elias Ashmole's** *Theatrum Chemicum Britannicum* **(1652).**

Constantine's conversion was another re-set for the world. The learning of the past was all brought under the mantle of Christianity and the authority of the Church.

The Roman world was notoriously regimented – we find the same city-plans and mosaic-designs at sites in Morocco, Germany and Bulgaria – but more diversity prevailed at grass-roots level, in people's private and communal lives. For the most part, moreover, it was tolerated. Cruel persecutions of the Christians did take place at times of crisis, when they made a convenient scapegoat, but for the most part the Emperors were content to live and let live.

A Ferment of Faiths

The cult of Mithras, Iranian god of the sun and war, was widely followed; so were those of Anatolian Cybele (whom the Romans identified with Ceres, their own goddess of the harvest) and of the Mesopotamian war-goddess known variously as Ishtar, Ananna and Astarte. The Christians themselves were divided between those who adhered to the account of their faith laid out in the scriptural sources and those 'gnostics' (from *gnosis*, the Greek for 'knowing') whose more mystic take was shaped by ancient Jewish writings themselves influenced by even earlier Mesopotamian sources. They shared with Persian Zoroastrianism – and, indeed, the other Middle Eastern religions – a 'dualistic' belief in a universe in which light and darkness, good and evil, contended eternally. And equally: official Christianity would ultimately condemn such dualism as heretical because it didn't see the benevolent force of God and his son Jesus as necessarily trumping the Devil's power.

... And Philosophies

Such was the stew of faith and philosophy that bubbled away in the Roman Empire in the early centuries CE. All these beliefs influenced and were influenced by each other. It's the same easy-going intellectual environment Forster found in Greek Alexandria. All the evidence is that theological thought and proto-scientific enquiry continued to flourish in that city and that Egypt's scholars still led the Empire at this time.

Few original manuscripts have survived from this time, but those which have contain a familiar cocktail of quasi-scientific observation, wild speculation, religious prayers and magic spells. Known collectively as the 'Greek Magical Papyri', these documents are indeed mostly written in Greek, though some are in Old Coptic and Demotic (both simplified forms of Egyptian hieroglyphic script). Their dating is uncertain, but all seem to have been written some time in either the first century BCE or the first century CE.

Mithras' cult was important in its own right in the history of Rome, but it was also a key conduit for older mysticisms of the east.

Her chariot drawn by lions, Cybele was an ancient Anatolian goddess whose influence flowed into the cultural crucible that was the Roman empire. This representation is from much later, c. 1509.

Sinful Simon

The creation of a clear demarcation between religion and magic is signposted in the story of Simon Magus in the Christian Bible (Acts 8, 9–24). A successful sorcerer in Samaria, Simon had, we're told, 'long amazed' the people there with his feats of magic. All agreed that he was 'rightly called the Great Power of God'. Even so, he'd recognized the superior powers of Christ's apostle Philip as he moved amongst the Samaritans working miracles and making converts. He had himself baptised then followed Philip around as he went about his ministry, marvelling at the wonders he saw him working. Saints Peter and John now arrived: they placed their hands on people's shoulders so they could receive the Holy Spirit. Simon envied them their power and wanted it for himself. He offered Peter money, but he angrily spurned it – and a false disciple who thought he could buy the grace of God. The name 'simony' was later given to the sin of those priests who tried to secure a superior position in the Church by bribery.'

Fragmentary Wisdom

The texts are mostly short – and frequently no more than fragments – and cover every subject under the sun. The sun itself is often invoked, indeed, as supreme deity – or just as the *symbol* of a supreme God, because this worldview seems to have incorporated the monotheistic Judaeo-Christian scheme into its own more pluralistic vision. Syncretism seems to have been second nature in this period, we've already seen. Hence, a spell for success in love suggests that Aphrodite – the Greek goddess of love, equivalent to the Roman Venus – be approached under her less familiar and consequently more mysterious Egyptian guise:

> Aphrodite's name which becomes known to no one quickly is 'NEPHERIEKI'. This is the name. If you wish to win a woman who is beautiful, be pure for three days, make an offering of frankincense, and call upon this name over it. You approach the woman and say it seven times in your soul as you gaze at her, and in this way it will succeed. But do this for seven days.

Naturally, in these pre-scientific times, no one thought to record whether this spell worked. Still we see the indissolubility of what would later be separated out into science, religion and magic. Significantly, though, we also see the relegation of the ancient Egyptian gods and goddesses, the mainstream deities here for so many centuries, to a secondary, secret, 'underground' status. And consequently, however, the promotion of their worship as a creed of the occult.

A lengthy prayer, the 'Mithras Liturgy', conflates the Persian god with Psyche (Greek goddess of the soul) and Providentia (the Roman one of destiny). It begs for immortality – 'not for gain but for instruction'. The speaker, endowed with this divine power, will rise up spiritually and be in a position to survey the entire universe and the whole vast sweep of time. 'I conjure you, holy light, holy brightness ...', starts another spell with echoes of Middle-Eastern dualistic thinking. Another offers a formula for summoning up Horus, ancient Egyptian god of the sun, sky, healing and personal protection. The preparations are elaborate, as would be expected for so ambitious an undertaking – but the charm to keep him there, once he's arrived, could hardly be more simple:

The Greek 'magical papyri' were a confusing cornucopia of knowledge, in several different languages – and in what we would see as wildly disparate fields of learning.

When he comes in, after greeting him, step with your left heel on the big toe of his right foot, and he will not go away unless you raise your heel from his toe, and at the same time say the dismissal.

From the sublime to the faintly ridiculous: a spell for ensuring that your horse wins a race involves writing down this prayer – 'Give me success, charm, reputation, glory in the stadium' – with a bronze stylus on 'the wide part of its hoof'.

A parting of the ways as St Peter sets a clear boundary between his orthodox Christianity and the magically-informed wisdom of Simon Magus. (Benozzo Gozzoli, Italy, fifteenth century.)

Pseudo-Silver

Some slightly later papyri, now held by the universities of Leiden (Netherlands) and Stockholm (Sweden), seem to date from some time in the third century CE. Their authorship is obscure, but they may have been written by one or more of the anonymous scholars at that time writing under the purported identity of the early Greek philosopher Democritus (*c.* 460–370 BCE) and consequently known now as 'Pseudo-Democritus'. (The Greek word 'pseudo' meant 'false' or 'fake'.) Fakeness was central to their science, indeed. A formula for 'the manufacture of silver' from the Leiden Papyri tells the reader to

> Buy charcoal which the smiths use and soften it in vinegar one day. After that, take one ounce of copper, soak it thoroughly in alum, and melt it. After that, take eight ounces of mercury but pour out the mercury thus measured into a secretion of poppy juice. Take also one ounce of silver. Put these materials together and melt; and when you have melted them, put the lumps so formed in a copper vessel with the urine of a pregnant animal and iron filing dust for three days. And the singular cloudiness which you will get on taking out is a sign of the natural fluctuation by which the mixture finds itself of equal composition by weight.

This isn't really the 'manufacture' of silver, of course: this substance actually has silver in it so might better be characterized as the creative adulteration of silver – or, at best, the manufacture of 'pseudo-silver'. As are other formulas suggested; the one, for instance, that recommends that the reader

> Purify white tin four times and melt together six parts of this and 1 mina of white Galatian copper; rub off and make what you wish.

'It will be silver of the first quality,' the author insists, 'except' (he adds disarmingly) 'that artisans can notice something peculiar about it because it is formed by the procedure mentioned.' Other personifications of 'Pseudo-Democritus' offered methods of making artificial gemstones, along with less controversial advice on ways of dyeing wool.

Growing Gold

It's tempting to write 'the manufacture of silver' off as straightforward forgery and, as we've seen, the element of fraud was to be intrinsic to alchemy as it emerged. It's only fair to point out, though, that the precise constitution of the main metals hadn't yet been nailed down firmly. The early alchemists appealed to Aristotle as their authority for the claim that all metals were ultimately one, which gradually refined itself as it matured until it became pure gold. The Greek philosopher hadn't quite said this, in fact, but he had, in his *Meteorologica* ('Meteorology', *c.* 340 BCE), suggested that metals 'grew' in the ground, like living organisms.

An architectural metaphor: Rome's Basllica di San Clemete al Laterano stands atop a pre-Christian sanctuary of Mithras, dating from the second century CE.

Democritus, depicted here by the Dutch artist Hedrick ter Brugghen (1628), had been an important Greek proto-scientist. A succession of imposters were subsequently to claim his name.

The sun, the origin of everything, he explained, heated up the earth, causing it to emit 'exhalations'. Some were dry, producing fossils beneath the soil. (Later, Aristotle would realize that the seashells and other objects found in rock deposits were the same as those that appeared on the seashore; for now, though, he saw them as an entirely separate thing.) Other exhalations were moist, and produced the vapours and the rain-showers, frost and snow that made up so much of what was thought of as the 'weather'. Beneath the earth's surface, though, they produced veins of metal, he believed. Of all these, gold was the only one typically found in its native state, not alloyed or mixed with other substances in ore, so it made sense to see it as metal in its purest form.

Again, Aristotle doesn't appear to have claimed that all metals would one day spontaneously develop into pure gold form, but his argument does at least leave that conclusion open. It was of course a convenient one for alchemists to come to. Whether honestly, but in wishful thinking, or in a cynical calculation of the benefits to be had from persuading a gullible public that their ersatz gold and silver might really be the real thing.

Help from Hades

Another Pseudo-Democritus claims to have been left in the lurch by the death of his master and mentor while they were still in the midst of their investigations into matter. He tried everything, working through every stage systematically, but couldn't quite bring his researches to their right conclusion. It appears to have gone without saying that he would now decide to try to summon up his teacher from the afterlife. The old man appeared to him, but only for long enough to tell him that the authorities in the realm of death didn't allow souls to communicate information with the living. Instead, he confided that he would find what he was looking for in his magic books that were waiting for him, somewhere in the Temple. Pseudo-Democritus, buoyed, had gone to the shrine and searched it from top to bottom – but, unfortunately, without result. Suddenly, in the secret heart of the Temple, a pillar had spontaneously opened up, revealing the books his master had hidden there. Opening these up, he pored over them tirelessly but could found nothing that he'd missed in his unsuccessful search. Finally, though, he stumbled on a saying he hadn't seen before: 'Nature delights in nature; nature conquers nature; nature masters nature.' It seemed to sum up the whole of his investigative work.

Tomus sextus operum.

ARISTOTELIS STAGIRITAE,

PERIPATETICORVM PRINCIPIS,
Naturalis eam Phylosophiæ adferens sectionem,

QVAE AD METEOROLOGICORVM,
seu sublimium corporum, & vegetabilium quidditates
species, & passiones, Animalium vero
Historiam, partes, & Incessum
spectare dignoscitur.

CVNCTA VSQVE AD EO CLARA, NITIDA,
Illustrata, distinctaq; prodeunt vt Aristotelem, Auerroemq;
ipsum, viuentes hæc disserere videatur.

QVAE HOC CLAVDVNTVR TOMO
sequens indicat pagina.

Cum summi Pontificis, Gallorum Regis, Senatusq; Veneti decreto.
VENETIIS MDLX.

The frontispiece to a 1560 Latin edition of *Meteorologica*, in which Aristotle argued that metals 'grew' organically in the ground.

'Chia Tzu-Lung Finds the Stone'. In Chinese tradition, this scholar had found a stone that turned tile or brick to silver. Eastern alchemy followed a parallel path to the Western brand.

A dramatic note to end on, but an enigmatic one as well, given that this Pseudo-Democritus doesn't tell us what the outcome of his investigation was. Of course, alchemical writing was always to revel in such ambiguity. The charitable explanation would be that this was because it hinted at the deeper paradoxes underlying the art – and indeed informing all existence; a more cynical one, that it enabled them to pull the wool over naïve readers' eyes.

An Eastern Alternative

Chinese alchemy appears to have evolved entirely independently of the Western discipline as an aspect of that religious and intellectual tradition known as Daoism or 'The Way'. Central to this school of thought was the belief that an overarching natural order underpins every sphere of existence, from the cosmic to the ethical, an order of two-in-one push–pull harmony, of *Yin* and *Yang*. Despite these differences, Chinese research offered intriguing parallels to the alchemy then emerging in the West. As outlined in early texts like the *Cantong qi* ('Book of the Kinship of the Three', by Wei Boyang, second century CE), its primary aim was to attain eternal life, to which end its practitioners strove tirelessly to produce elixirs.

As in Alexandria, and subsequently in Europe, alchemists saw the purification of metals as a means of achieving this: super-refined gold was sought as the basis for the *xiandan* ('pill of immortality'). But other materials were used as well: mercury, in the form of cinnabar, and rare animal products like rhinoceros horn. So too was *Qigong*, a regime of exercise, meditation and martial arts and the study of *wuxing* or the 'Five Agents'. The first five things were the planets Jupiter, Saturn, Mercury, Mars and Venus, but these quickly came to be identified with five elements (Fire, Water, Wood, Metal, Earth). And the five organs of the body: the Heart, Liver, Spleen, Lungs and Kidneys. The relations and reactions between all these different forces was readily encompassed by the dynamic two-in-one push–pull harmony of the *Yin* and *Yang*. Chinese alchemy was, accordingly, much more broadly conceived than its Western equivalent, which has enabled it to endure to some extent as a going concern into more recent times.

A Tangled Timeline

Establishing a clear chronology for alchemy's early history is maddeningly difficult. The idea of scientific 'progress' had not yet been born; antiquity bestowed authority, so writers strove to create the impression that the sources they cited were older than they really were. It's accordingly very difficult to know when the figure known as Hermes Trismegistus arrived on the Alexandrian scholarly scene. Works attributed to him (so known as *Hermetica*) include books on astronomy and astrology – and associated medical practices – believed to have been authored as early as the third century BCE.

內照圖

心者君主之官也，神明出焉，肺者相傅之官，治節出焉，肝者將軍之官，謀慮出焉，膽者中正之官，決斷出焉，膻中者臣使之官，喜樂出焉，脾胃者倉廩之官，五味出焉，大腸者傳道之官，變化出焉，小腸者受盛之官，化物出焉，腎者作強之官，伎巧出焉，

腦者髓之海，諸髓皆屬之，故上至泥丸下至尾骶，俱腎主之。膻中在兩乳間為氣之海，能分布陰陽為生化之源，故名曰海。膈膜在肺下與脊腹周回相著，如幕以遮濁氣，使不薰蒸上焦。幽門在大小腸之間，津液滲入膀胱，滓穢流入大腸變化出矣。

A map of the body geared to *Qigong* or 'Life Energy Cultivation', the effort to mirror the harmony of the universe within the human frame. Chinese alchemical thought has influenced thinking on health into modern times.

The Jade Emperor personifies purity for the Chinese religion of Daoism which has incorporated older alchemical teachings on universal harmony and order.

There's actually no certainty that Hermes Trismegistus ('Hermes the Thrice-Great') even existed. No mortal could have possessed his purported powers. He was said to have combined those of the Greek god Hermes (divine messenger and mediator between gods and men) with those of Thoth (the ibis-headed Egyptian god of wisdom and magic). So rapidly, moreover, did his reputation mount and the store of writings attributed to him grow over the course of the first millennium CE, that it becomes impossible to pin him down to any single time. In the early centuries of alchemy, he became a catch-all for a whole tradition and scores of supposed works were laid at his door.

Hermetic Definitions

Definitions of Hermes Trismegistus to Asclepius appears to have been published in the first century CE. Asclepius was the classical god of medicine, of course. The book is, as its title suggests, a list of 'definitions', though we might be more inclined to see them as aphorisms. 'Just as soul keeps up the figure while being within the body, which cannot possibly be constituted without a soul,' reads one; 'likewise all of the visible cannot possibly be constituted without the invisible.'

Hermes Trismegistus follows Empedocles in listing his elements as Earth, Air, Fire and Water but adds another in *Nous* – reason and knowledge but also the God that confers order and intelligibility on everything. Nous was never created, but the creator of all; 'the invisible good' which speaks to the 'soul' – the animating force of every body and eternal essence of mortal man. 'To Nous, nothing is incomprehensible.' Whenever man speaks with reason it is because he has been endowed with that gift by God.

Emerald Enigma

Just as difficult to date with any certainty is Hermes Trismegistus' most famous work, the *Emerald Tablet*, no text for which has been found dating back before the ninth century. That one, written in Arabic, may for all we know have been the original rather than the translation it was said to be. It was found appended to an Arabic text: Balinus' *Book of the Secrets of Creation.* But Balinus wrote as 'Apollonius of Tyana', borrowing the name from a Greek philosopher of the first century CE. Another author seeking to boost his credibility by exaggerating his writing's age. Many believed that it was even older, having been written, it was confidently claimed, many centuries before, at the dawn of time. Again, that impulse to canonize texts by pushing back their date of publication. Again, that chaotic chronology that has so perplexed modern historians.

The *Tablet*'s first appearance in Latin didn't come till almost 400 years later and this was translated in around 1680 by Isaac Newton. Truth, certainty, seem to be the subject of the text: 'Tis true without lying, certain & most true,' writes Newton:

> That which is below is like that which is above, and that which is above is like that which is below.

Echoing Plato's philosophy of forms, of the division between real and ideal, the thought chimes too with Christian and Muslim religious thinking about the relationship between Heaven and Earth. But both realms, for Hermes (again in Newton's words), 'do the miracles of one only thing', this one thing, presumably, being Nous:

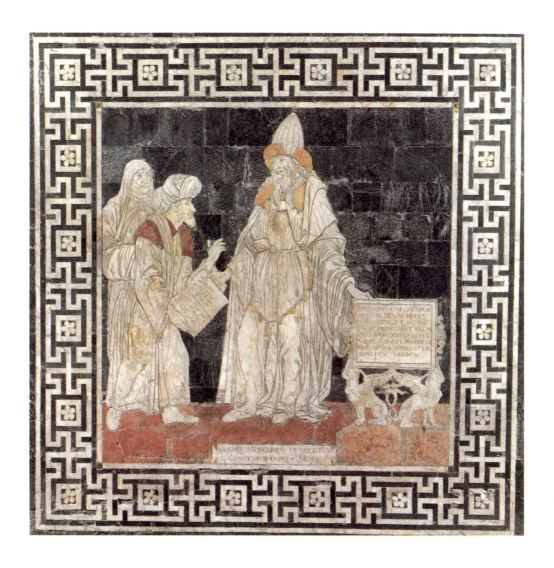

Dating from 1488, this representation of Hermes Trismegistus in mosaic in the floor of Siena's Cathedral reminds us how closely alchemy tracked 'official' Christian teaching in the West.

Hans Vredman de Vries painted this alchemist's laboratory in Hamburg, 1595.
The kneeling figure underlines the extent to which alchemy could still be seen
as an aspect of Christian worship.

> And as all things have been & arose from one by the mediation of one: so all things have their birth from this one thing by adaptation.

'The Sun is its father,' the text continues; 'the moon its mother, the wind hath carried it in its belly, the earth is its nourse.' That it's sexually engendered by the Sun and Moon appears to be important to Hermes Trismegistus; but so too is the role played by the other elements in its bringing-forth. The work of the alchemist in teasing out these different elements is key to knowledge and to glory, he goes on:

> Separate thou the earth from the fire, the subtile from the gross sweetly with great indoustry. It ascends from the earth to the heaven & again it descends to the earth & receives the force of things superior & inferior.

The prize, for the successful researcher, will be that of comprehending all the workings of the world, gaining unlimited power – and, apparently more important, unlimited fame:

> By this means you shall have the glory of the whole world & thereby all obscurity shall fly from you.

Cleopatra the Chrysopoeian

Alchemy is often caricatured as consisting solely in the quest to 'turn base metal into gold' but this – in Greek *chrysopoeia* – was only one of its early aims. It was, however, an object firmly in the sights of Cleopatra the Alchemist, who lived some time in the third century BCE so shouldn't be confused with the celebrated Ptolemaic queen (*c.* 70–30 BCE).

You were *meant* to confuse her with Queen Cleopatra, of course. Again the frantic effort to present her work as more antique – so more august – than it really was. It was so much the better that she was also easily confused with Cleopatra the Physician, an influential female medical writer of the first century CE (who also was almost certainly not really named Cleopatra!) The identity of Cleopatra the Chrysopoeian has just about always been unknown. She (if she *was* she; if she was even just one single person) sums up the complexity and ambivalence of early alchemy.

But the bamboozling ended there. Cleopatra appears to have been admirably down-to-earth and practical in the way she actually carried out at work. Resourceful too. She is said to have invented the alembic, for distilling fluids, as well. Reports in the later literature insist on the exactitude with which she weighed and measured out ingredients and the meticulousness with which she recorded all her findings so as to be able to replicate them in the future. There's still no sign of 'scientific method' here, but the need to be methodical was certainly being recognized.

Women's Work?

Maria the Jewess, who lived in Alexandria at some time between the first and third centuries CE, was reputed to have been as great an innovator as Cleopatra the Alchemist. Like her, she introduced new items of apparatus; like her, she was eminently practical in her approach, concerned to quantify, record and replicate with the utmost accuracy. She seems to have been more of a theorist, though, reviving the ancient Mesopotamian idea that substances were somehow gendered, 'male' materials bonding best with 'female' ones.

Many writers of the Christian era seem to have felt at least a symbolic connection between the extraction of metals from the earth with the birthing process – just as the Sumerians had, of course. More misogynistic connections were made as well. Metalworking, with its flames, its searing heat, its noisy hammering, and its association with the darkness 'down below', was widely seen as being somehow infernal. The *Book of Enoch*, an apocalyptic Jewish text from the fourth century BCE, had suggested that the skills of smelting metal had been passed to the world's women by the angels who fell from Heaven with the rebellious Satan. The idea would be picked up six centuries later by Zosimos of Panopolis:

Hermes Trismegistus, from *Stolcius*, Viridarium Chymicun, (1624).

This distilling furnace was built around 1500 by the German alchemist Hieronymus Brunschwig. The basic designs for such equipment had reputedly been established long before by Cleopatra the Chrysopoeian and Maria the Jewess.

> The ancient and divine writings say that the angels became enamoured of women; and, descending, taught them all the works of nature. From them, therefore, is the first tradition, *chema*, concerning these arts; for they called this book *chema* and hence the art of alchemy takes its name.

As Meredith K. Ray has pointed out, the view of alchemy as essentially feminine endured into early-modern times, even if it became increasingly symbolic as the centuries went on. The overwhelming majority of practitioners were male, of course, but they did not forget that women transformed materials day-by-day when cooking in their kitchens. And were they not responsible for the greatest transformation of them all when they gestated their husbands' babies in their wombs?

A Mystic Art

We know what we do about Cleopatra and Maria from the writings of Zosimos of Panopolis, who came after them at the beginning of the fourth century and was generous in his compliments about their work. He was less so about another Egyptian female alchemist, Paphnutia the Virgin, who appears to have been his contemporary but whose abilities he disdained. Or affected to: she would have been his rival, after all. Panopolis was a Greek colony beside the Nile near what is now Akhmim in Upper Egypt (upriver from the Delta region), though he seems to have spent his working life in Alexandria.

Zosimos of Panopolis helped 'keep alchemy honest' (at least inasmuch as anyone did) by insisting on its relationship with religious mysticism.

Most of his (voluminous) writings have been lost, but we know that he was a gnostic in his beliefs and that he saw his work as an extension of this. There were, he argued, two sorts of knowledge and two wisdoms: those of the Egyptians and those of the Jews. The second, he said, had been confirmed by God when he sent his son to earth. The Gnostics didn't deny the Gospels but they took comparatively little interest in them, seeing them rather as a springboard for their flight into more mystic realms of thought. Christ, after all, had been 'the Word made flesh' (John 1, 14), but they were interested in transcending the flesh; and, indeed, in soaring beyond the world itself. The wisdom of the Egyptian and Jewish mystics appealed to Zosimos precisely because 'it is not concerned with material and corruptible bodies', sustained only 'by prayer and divine grace'.

The pursuit of alchemy, he believed, set out 'to cleanse and save the divine soul bound in the elements' and 'free the divine spirit from its mixture with the flesh'. In other words, we studied materiality so as to find a way of escaping from it, through a mystic transformation into our purest form.

> As the sun is, so to speak, a flower of the fire and (simultaneously) the heavenly sun, the right eye of the world, so copper when it blooms – that is when it takes the colour of gold, through purification – becomes a terrestrial sun, which is king of the earth, as the sun is king of heaven.

Alexandria and the Arabs

Despite his name, Stephanus of Alexandria spent his most productive years in Constantinople, capital of what was still a glittering Byzantine Empire. An important writer on philosophy, he followed Plato's idealist line – one which of course sat well with the sort of mysticism espoused by gnostic writers like Zosimos.

And that of a new breed of Muslim writers. Islam had irrupted on to the international scene out of nowhere (which is what the deserts of Arabia were seen as) in the final decades of the seventh century. Its early years were a story of continuous war and conquest. Behind the violent front line, however, a new and dazzling civilization quickly took shape as the Arabs soaked up the art and culture of their conquered territories then took them off in their own direction.

Chrysopoea of Cleopatra.

Khalid ibn Yazid (*c.* 665–704) is a case in point. He had been born into the Arab elite, as grandson of Mu'awiya (*c.* 602–80), founder and first Caliph of the Umayyad Dynasty. As a young man, the story goes, Khalid is said to have left Damascus, the Umayyad capital, for Alexandria, where he met Stephanus and asked him to be his mentor. A more colourful story has him suddenly by some divine power receiving a book about the secrets of the Philosopher's Stone. Baffled by its contents, he offered a rich reward for assistance in understanding it. A horde of alchemists rushed in with promises of help. All to no avail, Khalid quickly came to realize that these supposed scholars were no more than self-seeking frauds. Finally, a Christian monk, Morienus, a hermit from far out in the Egyptian desert, presented himself at his door in Alexandria. Morienus elucidated the secrets of the volume for him, before taking himself off back to his desert cell without waiting for his reward. Khalid had the shysters executed and set out to pursue his studies alone, though Morienus is said to have reappeared at intervals to help him with particular difficulties.

Though undoubtedly fanciful, this anecdote is interesting because, whilst underlining alchemy's way of attracting the unscrupulously opportunistic, it also points up the bond that was taken to exist between 'true' mystics. This bond united pure-spirited enquirers like the Muslim Khalid and the Christian Morienus – and the gnostic Zosimos – transcending the specifics of their different faiths.

Spiritual Matter

Like the charlatans who flocked around Khalid, so eager to transmute his longing for the truth to gold, alchemy has all too often striven to conform to its own caricature. So it has been with the story of the so-called 'Philosopher's Stone'. This mysterious object is popularly seen as a quasi-magical tool with which base metal could be zapped and turned to gold or with whose shavings a tincture of eternal life could be created. But if it was popularly and stereotypically seen that way, that view was actively promoted by the more cynical majority of alchemists. It's on the basis of his promise to produce the Philosopher's Stone that Ben Jonson's Subtle gets so much money out of his wealthy mug Sir Epicure Mammon.

The reality was different. Or, rather, it wasn't: the reality was fake and fraudulent. But the *ideal*, to put it Platonically, was very different. The Philosopher's Stone, which started to feature in alchemical discussions from around the middle of the first millennium, was more what we might call a philosophical 'construct'. Rather like the unitary mysticism that brought men like Zosimos, Khalid and the fabled Morienus together, transcending the doctrinal details of their respective faiths, alchemical thinkers proposed the existence of some ultimate substance that would somehow embody the essence of matter without being burdened by the secondary characteristics of specific materials. In other words, it was matter made spirit – hence its extraordinary elusiveness; and its calculatedly incommunicative labelling as 'The Philosopher's Stone'.

The idea of enlightenment as a mountain to be scaled is familiar from everything from Hindu tradition to Dante's Purgatorio. It made a natural metaphor for the alchemists' progression to the Philosopher's Stone.

Jabir ibn Hayyan, 'Geber', was a towering presence in medieval alchemy on both sides of the Muslim–Christian divide.

The Genius of Geber

Jabir ibn Hayyan (by tradition *c.* 730–*c.* 810), known in medieval Christendom just as 'Geber', came from Tus. This city lay in what was then the Umayyad province of Khurasan and is now in the northeast corner of Iran. He was himself an Arab, a child of the region's Islamic conquerors. That's if he actually existed at all, for he's that familiar figure in alchemy's early history, an eminence who appears as like as not to be a composite of several different authors.

Perhaps a great many, because over 200 works have been attributed to him (3,000 in some accounts), on subjects ranging from botany to grammar, from pharmacology to astronomy, but centring on the philosophy and practice of alchemy. Many have believed he was responsible for the first Arabic translation of the *Emerald Tablet* tacked on to the end of Balinus' *Book of the Secrets of Creation*, but there's very little evidence either way. Modern researchers who are prepared to accept that such an individual as Jabir actually existed tend to think he did so significantly later than traditionally assumed, in the tenth century.

Like Khalid ibn Yazid 200 years or more before, Jabir is said to have benefited from the mentoring he received from a Christian monk, Morienus. (The historiographical timeline of alchemy in this period is as ever-shifting as the Saharan sand.) It's fair to say, though, that Islamic scholars did derive much wisdom from their readings in a Christian literature largely written by monks and that we have no real reason to doubt that eager students sought out learning wherever they could find it, across religious lines.

Medicine for Metal

Jabir became famous for his elegant demonstration in the *Book of Clarification* that all metals were compounds of either mercury (or quicksilver) or sulphur. This was by no means a new idea, having been advanced by Balinus and deriving ultimately from Aristotle's theory of exhalations, mercury being the moist and sulphur the dry. 'The metals', Jabir tells us,

> are all of the substance of quicksilver coagulated with the mineral sulphur that rises into it in a smoky exhalation of the earth. They differ only in their accidental qualities which depend upon the different forms of sulphur which enter into their composition. For their part, these sulphurs depend upon the different earths and their exposure in the heat of the sun. The most subtle, pure, and balanced sulphur is the sulphur of gold. This sulphur coagulates quicksilver with itself in a complete and balanced manner. On account of this balance, gold withstands fires, remaining unchanged in it.

The other metals, it's implied, were products of less 'pure' and 'balanced' blends of mercury and sulphur. Jabir's reasoning obviously echoes Stephanus' account of the physical chemistry underlying metallurgy. More philosophically, though, it can be seen as analogous to the more mystic theories Stephanus would share with later writers like Zosimos and Khalid ibn Yazid.

Great alchemists of the past look down as workers busy themselves about the various tasks of the laboratory. An illuminated page from Norton's *The Ordinall of Alchemy*, 1477.

The red king stands for sulphur; his white-faced queen for mercury. So too does the green god Mercury, standing ready to join them in marriage as patron of the entire alchemical process.

A Mercurial Talent

The element we now call mercury, we've seen, was one half of the central opposition of existence, in Jabir's alchemical scheme, but Mercury was also the winged-footed messenger of the Roman gods. This of course made him their equivalent of the Greek divine herald Hermes – already well-established as an important figure for the alchemists and presumably the inspiration for Hermes Trismegistus' name. But the substance itself is of interest in its own right. Actually a metal, it's the only one to be in its molten state at normal temperatures – weirdly, it seems to be a liquid but not wet. So strong is the surface tension it produces that a drop retains its integrity when it's poured out on to a flat surface and then pushed around. This behaviour occasioned its earlier English name 'quicksilver' – 'quick' meant 'living'; it seemed 'silver' in its shiny whiteness.

Ouroboros (representation of a serpent eating its own tail) with the words ἕν τὸ πᾶν, hen to pān ('the all is one') from the Chrysopoeia of Cleopatra, in the 3rd or 4th century AD.

In Search of Equilibrium

As important as he was for his philosophical views, however, Jabir was very much a working alchemist, following women like Cleopatra the Chrysopoeian and Maria the Jewess in his methodical, meticulous approach. Jabir's theories have often been referred to as 'the science of the balance'. Taking a line through Hippocratic medicine, he sought to show that carefully-developed elixirs could 'heal' metals, transmuting them into truer, purer forms, by adjusting the balance between their different qualities of warmth and cold, dryness and moisture. The alchemist's all-important task was to balance out these influences in their right proportions, just as the doctor's was to achieve a stable equilibrium in the patient's body. Improbable? Yet again, we have to bear in mind that, outré as they may now sound to us, such views would be mainstream 'science' until the eighteenth century.

'All is Interrelated'

'All those who were well-informed about the *Franj* saw them as beasts superior in courage and fighting ardour but in nothing else, just as animals are superior in strength and aggression.' This remark by the Arab chronicler Usamar Ibn Munqidh (1095–1188) of the 'Frankish' or French Crusaders in the Middle East reminds us that the balance of power wasn't what it would subsequently become. That 'the West' enjoyed overwhelming superiority – not just in military might but in technological development and general know-how – has seemed self-evident for several centuries. It wasn't always so, however, and certainly wasn't in medieval times. Islamic culture was then far more sophisticated than that of the West. In addition to their own inherited traditions, the Muslim peoples had taken on ideas and aesthetic sensibilities from the countries they had conquered in western Asia – including, ironically, those of a classical Graeco-Roman culture largely lost to medieval Europe. To a considerable extent, even 'Western' wisdom came to Europe courtesy of the Islamic east.

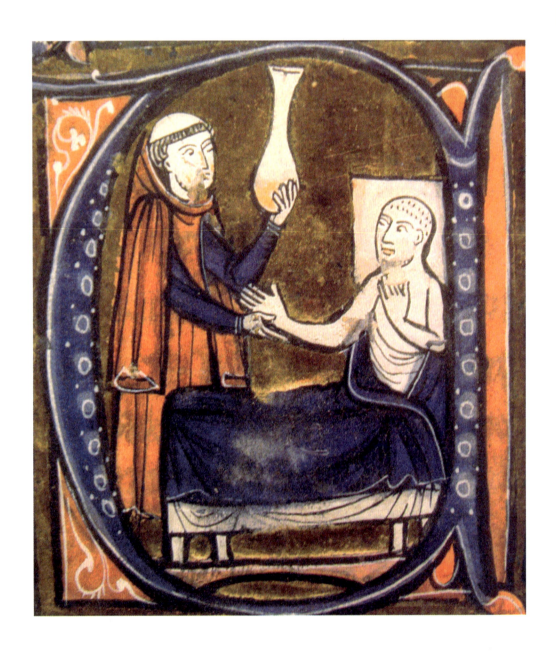

Muhammad ibn Zakariva Razi (865–925) was known as Rhazes in the West. This Persian polymath did important work on alchemy.

From Macedon to Spain

Sometimes by strange and devious routes. Supposedly a letter written by Aristotle to his student Alexander the Great, *Secretum Secretorum* ('The Secret of Secrets') had by all accounts been written originally in Greek. Whilst that text had long since disappeared, a Syriac translation seems to have survived. This had in its turn been translated into Arabic in the ninth century. As might be expected of a mentor's advice to a young prince, it included advice on statecraft, but ranged far beyond that into subjects from ethics and astrology to medicine and physiognomy (the art of reading character in faces). And, of course, alchemy.

In truth, modern scholars tell us, the *Secretum Secretorum* was never written by Aristotle in the first place, but a tenth-century Arabic original masquerading (in the now-familiar alchemical way) as something much more venerable. Yet it was still a conduit for ancient Greek ideas. It would be an exaggeration to claim that the Arabs were solely responsible for the survival of classical philosophy into medieval, and hence into modern, Europe: obscure scribes in far-flung monasteries were keeping these traditions just about alive. But it's true that the enthusiasm with which they seized on these ancient texts when they came upon them in the course of their conquests, and the energy with which they studied and translated them (along with innumerable works of pseudo-Aristotelianism and -Platoism) revived them as areas of active interest in the post-Crusading era.

Man of Mathematics

The English scholar Adelard of Bath (*c.* 1080–*c.* 1152) travelled in southern Italy and Sicily – areas recently under Muslim occupation – reading all the Arabic works he could about astronomy and science. He was to gain enormous influence, becoming tutor to his country's future King Henry II (1133–89). His version of the *Elements* of Euclid (*c.* 300 BCE), made from an Arabic text, is the first known translation into Latin of this famous geometry primer. Adelard is widely believed to have introduced Arabic numbering (1, 2, 3 ..., as opposed to Roman I, II, III, IV ...) to Europe. He also wrote extensively on astrology and alchemy.

Another front in the Crusades had of course been Spain, invaded by the Muslim Moors in 711, and still partly occupied into High Medieval times. A Muslim state, al-Andalus, would endure in the south until the end of the fifteenth century, though under mounting pressure from the Christian kingdoms to the north. In the twelfth century it was a flourishing centre. Despite outbreaks of fighting, there were lengthy periods of peace between, during which a brisk trade took place between the contending peoples. As did a cultural commerce: John of Seville (1100–80) was just one of several Castilian monks who made contact with Muslim scholars in al-Andalus and produced Latin translations of what he saw as important texts. These included commentaries on Aristotle by the noted Arab scholar Ibn Sina ('Avicenna', *c.* 980–1037) and in around 1120 at least sections of the *Secretum Secretorum*. All found eager readers in the monasteries of Western Europe.

The Persian prophet Zoroaster puts a pair of demons in their place in this image from a fifteenth-century edition of the *Secretum Secretorum*.

Adelard of Bath brings a couple of monkish students up to date with his innovations in mathematics. He translated Arabic works on alchemy as well.

'A Pearl of Great Price'

The *Secretum Secretorum* was crucial, though. It picked up from Jabir the idea that all matter derived from mercury and sulphur, calling for these conflicting forces to be made into a marriage of opposites. This union was symbolized by the image of an egg incubated by the so-called Hermes Bird and warmed by the blazing Egyptian sun. Seen from without, the egg looked like a pearl – pure, white and precious and in Christian scripture a symbol of the Kingdom of Heaven (Matthew 13). In the Arab-influenced alchemical writings it represented the strength and purity of the Philosopher's Stone.

Inwardly, it embodied the idea of opposing forces fusing. The clear mercury was the white of the egg, the sulphur its golden yolk. The two clung together in opposition as the basis for all life. The idea of the 'world egg' had obvious precedents in Egyptian and Greek mythology, but the *Secretum Secretorum* developed the idea. The folding together of yolk and white into a single form recalled the *Emerald Tablet*'s suggestion of the interchangeability of everything: 'That which is below is like that which is above, and that which is above is like that which is below.'

Or, as indeed some had translated the ambiguous Arabic phrase, 'That which is within is that which is without'. The egg was like a womb, which – as the Mesopotamian metalworkers had recognized – was like the earth. European alchemists called the bulbous vessel they warmed up their ingredients in the 'Philosophers' Egg' because they hoped that in it they'd be incubating the long-sought-after Philosopher's Stone. Some alchemists used the name 'Philosopher's Egg' where others said 'Philosopher's Stone', indeed, underlining the reflexive relationship between container and contained.

The Philosopher Friar

Acclaimed for his brilliance and breadth of learning, Roger Bacon (*c.* 1220–*c.* 1292) became known as 'Doctor Mirabilis' ('Marvellous Doctor') but held on to his humility as a Franciscan friar. Along with theology, he was an avid student of philosophy, language and physical chemistry. Whilst not inventing gunpowder (it had been used in China for several centuries), he was the first Westerner to record its formula. Like some pre-Renaissance Leonardo, he speculated about submarines, flying machines and vehicles which would make their own way, like a modern car. For the most part, though, he kept his scientific and philosophical feet firmly on the ground. His career underscores the closeness with which alchemy coexisted with what we would see as more legitimate fields of study.

By the same token, it illustrates how, as custodians of the wonders of religion, the Christian clergy were seen as natural proprietors for more occult ideas. The boundary between magic and religion, non-existent in ancient times, remained

The Hermes Bird stands amidst the seven feathers which pierce the waters from which it will be reborn. The feathers represent the seven planets and the seven metals. An image from the Ripley Scroll.

Engraving from *Symbola aureae* (1617) by Michael Maier, showing Roger Bacon.

decidedly permeable even now. As its title suggests, Bacon's *Letter on the Secret Workings of Art and Nature and on the Vanity of Magic* casts cold water on a lot of his alchemically minded contemporaries' claims, showing how the results they obtain can be explained by natural means. Even so, Bacon (if it *is* him: the *Letter*'s authorship is doubtful) offers advice on how to attain the Philosopher's Stone. Likewise, whilst he is openly dismissive of Hermes Trismegistus' claims to greatness, he implicitly acknowledges many of his doctrines. Quite where Bacon stood on the question of alchemy isn't clear: so many of 'his' writings probably weren't his, for one thing.

Talking Head

An extravagant mythology arose around Roger Bacon's reputation: he was one of several medieval alchemists said to have designed and built a 'Brazen Head'. This, by either magical or mechanical means, could move and talk, and even think and answer questions, a prototype, perhaps, for the later legend of the Golem, as it emerged in sixteenth-century Prague. Frankenstein's monster, as described by Mary Shelley (1797–1851) might be seen as a distant descendant – as, for that matter, might the modern-day computer.

The Medical Connection

Just as there appeared to be a 'natural' continuity between the mysteries of Christian theology and those of alchemy, so there seemed to be between those of medicine

and the occult. Several European monarchs had private physicians with sidelines (or much more) in alchemical research, including the Holy Roman Emperor Charles IV (1316–78), King Charles V of France (1338–80).

Urinary Tract

Today the search for the Philosopher's Stone is seen as a mythologically based metaphor for a dreamily romantic but inevitably doomed endeavour; very much like that for the Holy Grail. But the two quests appear to have been associated in the medieval mind as well. Reputedly the silver chalice or dish used by Christ at the Last Supper (Matthew 26), the Grail was, in Arthurian myth, kept in a castle at the end of the world. In some versions of the story – which was retold many times by different romancers – it was in the keeping of the 'Fisher King'. He was sickly, rendered sexually impotent by a wound, and his kingdom was dying all around him. Helpless as he was, all he could do was sit in a boat on the river near his castle and fish. One day, someone would come to him with the right question, and he would be healed and the Holy Grail released. Till then, it remained locked up – as did the Fisher King's barren lands. The questing knight could only retrieve the Grail by redeeming the realm of the Fisher King.

As Jonathan Hughes has noted, the *Commentarium urinarum*, by the French writer Walter de Agilon, weaves the two tropes together to dramatize the quest for perfect health. An instruction manual on uroscopy (the medicinally informed

Roger Bacon talks with his Brazen Head as imagined by the nineteenth-century English illustrator Harold Nelson in *The Famous History of Fryer Bacon*, 1895.

The Franciscan friar Berthold Schwarz (1318–84) was widely credited with the invention of gunpowder. He actually seems to be doing this in this engraving from 1880.

examination of the urine to assess a patient's health), it shows man battling the illnesses caused by imbalances of the humours which loom up in his path like the giants and monsters of chivalric myth. The prize will be a perfect equilibrium of red and white, in Christian terms the red of Jesus' Passion and the pure white of his sacred Grail; in bodily ones blood and phlegm. The former represents gentle warmth, the latter a clear, cool-headed calm. These will be our hero's defences against an excess of out-of-control choler (heat or anger) and melancholy bile. But they also represent the red heat of sulphur and the white chill of mercury, which – gendered masculine and feminine respectively – must be combined in perfect balance for the Philosopher's Stone.

A Capricious King

Edward III (1312–77) became England's king in 1327. His half-century reign was one of the longest in English royal history. Along with the aura of the alpha male he won with notable victories in war with the French, at Crécy (1346) and Poitiers (1356), went rumours of sexual excess which his subjects didn't find so appealing. The Black Death (1346–53) sat on the whole century like a deathly pall, while in the latter years of Edward's reign his physical decline made him something of a Fisher King for England. He is known to have been a patron to alchemists throughout his reign. Despite having had his own personal copy of *Secretum Secretorum*, his motivation appears to have been unabashedly mercenary: the gaining of gold for his chronically overstretched exchequer. If it was all right for the Church, why not for the monarchy?

Edward's most notorious commission, legend has it, was to the Catalan alchemist Ramon Lull (*c.* 1232–*c.* 1315). Lull was said to have succeeded in making the

Philosopher's Stone by grinding up pearls and reconstituting them on a far larger scale. This then equipped him to make great quantities of gold. The story goes that Edward summoned Lull to come and work for him in the Tower of London in the 1340s. Any gold he produced, he promised, would be used for pious purposes, funding a crusade. The alchemist had spectacular success, turning over 20 tons of lead and tin to gold – which Edward promptly spent on a campaign in France. Lull returned to the continent in disgust.

Royal Cults

None of this could actually have happened, of course, because Lull had died when Edward was three years old. The story is nevertheless revealing in highlighting the glamour and prestige the most famous alchemists had. If scholars seeking attention for their theories had learned to bring them out under other, more famous names (scores of such manuscripts were attributed to Lull himself), kings and their counsellors too wished to associate themselves with celebrated alchemists. Edward's advisers had in fact organized something of a 'personality cult' around their lord, promoting the idea that he was a sort of reborn King Arthur and his court a Camelot. The only thing then missing was a Merlin the Magician. Lull fitted the part; it scarcely mattered that it wasn't true.

A comparable cult was created around the figure of his grandson and successor, Richard II (1367–*c*. 1400). He was a fresh-faced boy of ten when he ascended the

Lady Intelligence shows Ramon Lull the Tree of Science – a sort of mind map of medieval knowledge. His alchemical researches were just one aspect of Lull's work.

A modern (1877) reinterpretation of a sixteenth-century engraving shows Ramon Lull with a salamander – symbol of fire and the transformation it could bring.

throne and his counsellors played on this to promote him in mythologized terms as an embodiment of the unicorn – pure, white, rare, and faintly feminine. (The unicorn was reputedly a wild and ungovernable beast, but it would meekly submit to the control of a virgin girl.) His personal emblem, the white hart (or stag), was vaguely reminiscent of the unicorn: its colour recalled that of the pure pearl. In alchemical terms, then, Richard was mercurial, where his aggressive, debauched grandfather had been sulphurous. Praise of Richard focused on his gentleness and chastity, notes historian Jonathan Hughes. Where Edward's admirers had presented the English court as Camelot, Richard's rebranded it as the New Jerusalem the Bible had promised (in the books of Ezekiel and Revelations), with the king himself as a Solomon in all his glory. And in his wisdom. Though draped in rich robes and festooned in gold and precious stones, Richard was always portrayed in a serious and prayerful posture and his deep familiarity with the lore of alchemy advertised. He even commissioned a *Libellus Geomancie* ('Little Book of Geomancy') to explore the possibilities of divination through tracing the energies operating within the earth as manifested in the natural shapes and patterns found in surface rock and soil.

Outlawed

Richard's unworldliness was real – so much so as to be his ultimate undoing. In 1399, he was overthrown by Henry Bolingbroke (*c.* 1367–1413), who took his

throne as Henry IV, and a year later had him murdered. So hostile was Henry to alchemy that he outlawed it with his 'Act Against Multipliers' of 1404. 'Multiplying' – making gold out of base metal – threatened to flood the market with false coin, he reasoned, undermining the economy and the authority of the Crown. Realizing that it might provide him with tax income, Henry VI (1421–71) licensed individual alchemists to operate, but the Act itself would not be repealed until 1688.

Whatever the rules on 'multiplying', the study of alchemy was never actually going to be suppressed as long as there was greed for gold – pretty much a given in any society. Or, for that matter, as long as there were enquiring minds, for the boundaries between 'true' science and 'false' occult investigation had even now to be definitively drawn. Hence the continuing interest among a great many serious-minded churchmen, amongst them George Ripley (*c.* 1415–90). An Augustinian canon, he was also personal physician to Edward IV (1442–83), and was indeed to be knighted for his services.

Opening the Gates

We've already seen that alchemy could have a pass-key to the innermost circles of royalty through the ministrations of such physicians. As a senior clergyman, Sir

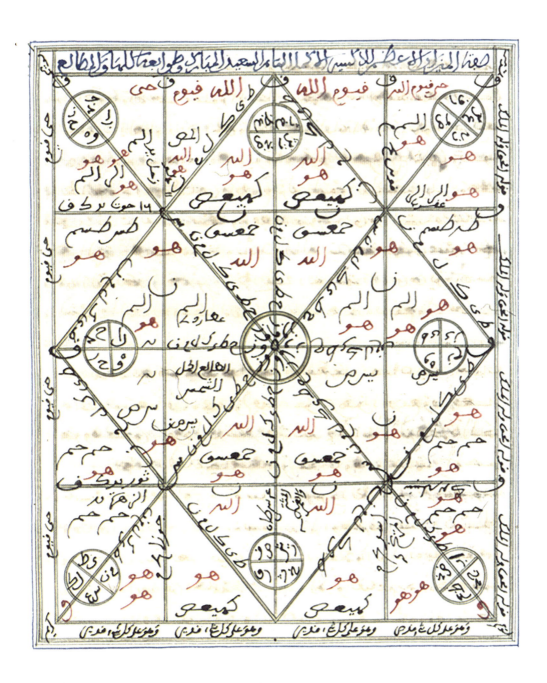

The Egyptian alchemist 'Izz al-Din al-Jaldaki produced this chart in the fourteenth century to set forth his theories on the importance of balance in science and nature.

**Thomas Norton was one of the most famous English alchemists of the Middle Ages.
He wrote a poem, The Ordinall of Alchemy (1477).**

George gave it a public voice as well. He does seem to have been entirely sincere in his pursuit of alchemical understanding and his desire to knit his findings in with what he believed as a Christian. His idea of 'exaltation', that metals progress through higher, more spiritual states on their way to perfection, echoes the views of earlier, more mystically minded writers like Stephanus, Zosimos, Morienus and Khalid. Sir George's most direct inspiration seems to have been Ramon Lull, whom he often references. The Catalan had set out a scheme by which the virtuous intellect ascended to enlightenment over a series of levels, like a ladder's rungs. It's hard for us to know how familiar Ripley was with the wider writings of the man himself, though: there were already works by scores of 'pseudo-Lulls' in circulation.

More lastingly important than any of his specific points, perhaps, is the fact that Ripley's book *The Compound of Alchemy; or, the Twelve Gates leading to the Discovery of the Philosopher's Stone* (1471) constitutes a major milestone in alchemy's journey towards becoming a true science. Not because it even comes close to passing muster from a modern point of view. Sir George is as innocent of 'scientific method' as Stephanus was. But he showed a real interest in opening

up his subject to free enquiry that reminds us of the Greeks, not just by writing in English but by doing so in verse.

Nothing that would give him any real title to membership of the canon of English literature, but reader-friendly and engaging all the same. Just as the religious mystics of medieval times – Lull himself, or England's own Richard Rolle (*c.* 1300–1349) and Walter Hilton (*c.* 1340–96), for instance – set out the inward journey to spiritual fulfilment as a series of discrete stages, he sees the quest for alchemical truth as leading through successive gates. Each is a particular process, to whose ins and outs he offers relatively detailed guidance. It's invariably approachable, even if it isn't always quite as transparent in its meaning as it seems to think it is.

Doggerel Details

The first 'gate' the reader has to go through, for example, is 'calcination', a process of slowly heating and gently stirring antimony to break it down. (Others will include 'solution', 'separation', 'conjunction', 'putrefaction' (the moment of blackening under heat, the substance's symbolic 'death') …) Generally speaking, calcination is done with the assistance of solvents – though Ripley has strong views on which ones should and shouldn't be employed:

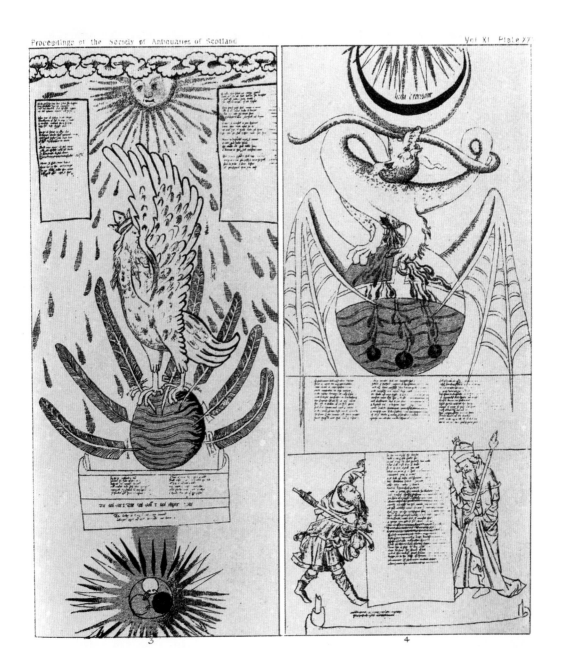

**Golden winged bird from the Ripley Scroll by 15th century alchemist, George Ripley.
This is one of 21 extant Ripley scrolls.**

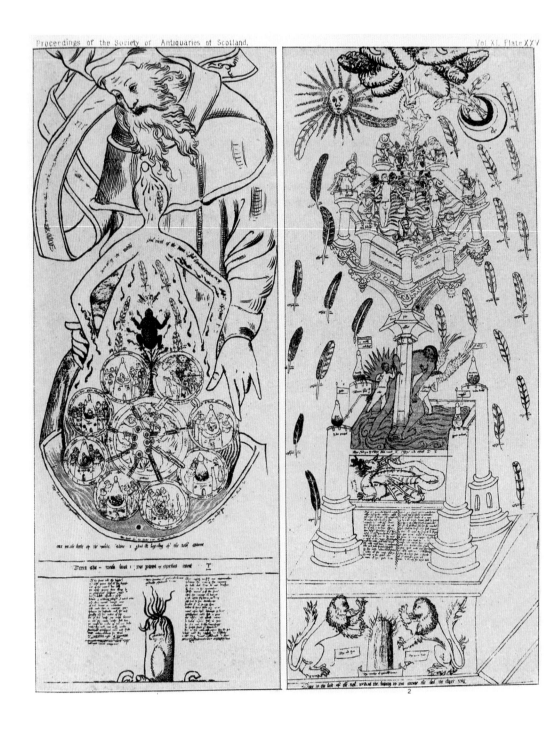

Alchemy illustrations in the Ripley scroll, housed in the Library of the Royal College of Physicians, Edinburgh. Presented to the College by the Earl of Cromarty in 1707.

> Calcination is the purgation of our stone,
>
> And restoration also of its natural heat.
>
> Of radical humidity it looseth none,
>
> Inducing solution into our stone most mete.
>
> Seek after philosophy I you advise
>
> But not after the common guise,
>
> With sulphur and salts prepared in diverse ways.
>
> Neither with corrosives, nor with fire alone,
>
> Nor with vinegar, nor with ardent water,
>
> Neither with the vapour of lead,
>
> Our stone is calcined according to our intent.
>
> All those who to calcining so be bent,
>
> From this hard science withdraw their hand,
>
> Till they our calcining better understand.

If the journey's stages suggest religious mysticism, the styling of the House of Philosophy as a 'castle' to be 'conquered' lends the story something of the air of a chivalric quest:

> You are now within the first gate,
>
> Of the castle where the Philosophers dwell.
>
> Proceed wisely that you may win,

> And go through more gates of that Castle.
>
> This Castle is round as any bell,
>
> And gates it has yet eleven more,
>
> One is conquered, now to the second go.

Quite how all this is supposed to mesh with the thinking laid out in 'Ripley's Wheel' isn't clear, but Ripley does appear to have been the creator of this cosmological design. Basically, it's a representation of the universe with the sun, moon and planets circling the earth (the work of Copernicus (1473–1543) was still a generation off), with their corresponding elements written in. The famous, fascinating 'Ripley Scroll', though quite possibly inspired by Ripley's writings, is not known to have any immediate connection with Sir George. As a visual expression of the wondrous richness and complexity of medieval alchemy, though, it is absolutely unequalled. The original is lost, but 23 copies still exist.

Hustler or Hero?

Georg Faustus (*c.* 1480–*c.* 1541) was a German alchemist, magician and astrologer. He was what English-speakers of his age had come to call a 'mountebank' (from the Italian *monta in banco!* – 'get up on the bench!') because he'd go from place to place, climbing up on a bench to address the crowds at busy fairs or markets. The name quickly came to be seen as synonymous with 'charlatan' – a huckster whose true knowledge or skills didn't match up to their persuasive patter. Beyond this,

A Three-Headed Monster in an Alchemical Flask, representing the composition of the alchemical Philosopher's Stone: Salt, Sulphur, and Mercury, by Edith Annie Ibbs (1863–1937) after Salomon Trismosin.

The sand in his hourglass all but exhausted now, Faust finally gets round to considering the skull before him and the message of mortality it holds for him.

almost nothing is known of the original Faust, but his story took on a legendary life of its own and soon it was widely said that he'd had spectacular skills, which he'd gained by selling his soul to the Devil. Satan gave him an infernal servant, Mephistophilis, whose job was to give him all he asked for – and then finally drag him down to hell. At first his tale was told with irreverent amusement, a popular subject for puppet-shows and farces.

The English playwright Christopher Marlowe (1564–93) adapted it as *Doctor Faustus* with (after a few slapstick scenes) a truly terrifying conclusion. But the German Johann Wolfgang von Goethe (1749–1832) produced the version that's most vividly remembered now. His *Faust* (published in two parts, 1808 and 1832) sees the character as an intrepid artist ready to brave all to transcend his human limitations. The gulf between Goethe's hero and the fifteenth-century swindler is enormous, but it arguably runs through the whole history of alchemy.

A New Era

The Renaissance ('Rebirth') of European culture is generally held to have started in around 1300 – or, by different experts, anything up to a hundred years later. By any calculation, it was old news by Ripley's time, but things had moved at different speeds in different countries, northern Europe lagging significantly behind the place it had all started, Florence, and Italy more generally. And, indeed, in different disciplines. Alchemy, we've seen, was simultaneously eager to advance and to hide that fact, making spurious claims to antiquity and constructing a chaotic chronological record around itself.

Hans Burgkmair (1473–1531) produced many admiring representations of the Holy Roman Emperor Maximilian I but doesn't appear to have approved of his alchemical enquiries.

The Flamboyant Physician

Even so, we get the sense of a real leap forward in the career of Paracelsus (Theophrastus von Hohenheim, *c.* 1493–1541). Born in Einsiedeln, northern Switzerland, the son of a physician and pharmacist, he'd studied medicine at Basel and Vienna then done his doctorate at Ferrara, Italy. Thereafter, he'd travelled widely, through Scandinavia, Spain and Portugal, England and across much of Eastern Europe, serving at times as an army surgeon in the Netherlands and Russia. Even when his travelling days were nominally over, he ended up moving frequently from place to place, his peripatetic lifestyle forced upon him by his apparent compulsion to burn bridges. He appears to have had no filter when it came to denouncing local doctors or criticizing other scholars' work.

If he was rebarbative with his contemporaries, his distinguished predecessors were not spared his scathing censure: he publicly burned texts by Galen and Avicenna . That said, he was contemptuous of certain aspects of alchemical tradition too. He had no time for *chrysopoeia*, though many people, then as now, assumed that the transformation of base metal into gold was the main point of alchemy. As far as he was concerned, the chief significance of alchemical enquiry was as a branch – and a subordinate one – of medicine.

A portrait of Paracelsus, presumed to be by the Flemish artist Quentin Matsys (1466–1530), shows a normal-looking north European – but with a certain shiftiness in his gaze.

Like his contemporary Martin Luther, Paracelsus clashed with senior churchmen who saw themselves as guardians of traditional scientific thinking. Here he argues his case in a court in Basel.

Iconoclastic Ideas

Sometimes, an upmarket mountebank, he'd promote his ideas at public lectures: his insistence on speaking German rather than Latin, for the understanding of ordinary people, was seen as subversive by his learned peers. Whilst it obviously echoed Ripley , it also chimed with the call Martin Luther (1483–1546) was making for religious reading and discussion to take place in the vernacular as part of the Reformation he'd launched at Wittenberg in 1517. In the same spirit of vernacularization, Paracelsus came up with a whole new herbal, using curative plants from northern Europe rather than the Mediterranean species Galen had (naturally) favoured.

Paracelsus deployed a radical rhetoric in calling for physicians to up their game. 'Destruction perfects that which is good,' he wrote, which sounds almost Nietzschean in its violence. Really, though, he was only calling for a greater rigour in analysis – which in its original Greek, of course, also means 'breaking down'. 'For the good', he continued,

> cannot appear on account of that which conceals it. The good is least good whilst it is thus concealed. The concealment must be removed so that the good may be able freely to appear in its own brightness. For example, the mountain, the sand, the earth, or the stone in which a metal has grown is such a concealment. Each one of the visible metals is a concealment of the other six metals.

Adding Salt

His strenuously methodical approach apart, Paracelsus' chief contribution to alchemy was the addition of a third element to the mercury–sulphur duo which had reigned supreme till now. Salt, he said, with the other two, made up the *Tria Prima* – the 'three first things' of which everything was composed.

He said everything and he meant it. Paracelsus saw physical geography, the weather, the structure of the universe as the products of chemical reactions. The basis of this relationship was what he believed to be a universal correspondence between the 'microcosm' and the 'macrocosm' – the small-scale universe and the full-scale one around it. The pre-eminent microcosm was the human body: it paralleled (and was paralleled by) the structure of the cosmos as a whole. They shared an ultimate destiny as well. Just as the physical creation would eventually be purified into spirit, so the soul would leave behind the body in Final Resurrection at world's end.

Purified itself, the *tria prima* could be used to separate out the elements composing any other substance then recombine them in their purest and most spiritual form. Controversially, he argued that this could apply to toxins, which could be made safe by purification then used as medicines. Unfortunate patients were treated with everything from antimony to arsenic: many must have been further sickened or even killed. Despite this, Paracelsus was overall a progressive force, something of a one-man Renaissance in medicine.

The fictive sage Senior explains to young Adolphus how the Tree of Metals works. The points of the lower triangle are the *Tria Prima*. From *Occulus Philosophia* (Frankfurt, 1613).

An old king must drown in the background for a new king to be crowned. Salomon Trismosin's *Splendor Solis* ('Splendour of the Sun', c. 1580) revolves around cycles of death and rebirth.

Back to Life

The sheer ambition of Paracelsianism was impressive. The sky was the limit: carrying the macro/micro idea to extremes, Paracelsus (or, perhaps more likely, one of his 'Pseudos') even proposed that a chemical reaction might be conceived to create a homunculus. This 'miniature man' would have his adult cognitive faculties fully formed even if his body was only the size of a child's. Indeed, there was no reason (the Paracelsians argued) why he should not have his brain pre-loaded with all the skills and learning he could possibly need. Better still, because he was artificially created, he might be brought into the world without the involvement of woman, with all the frailty and folly that entailed, his blood completely free of female taint.

All but the most crazily dedicated of Paracelsus' followers realized that making a homunculus might be just too tall an order. They settled for the attempt to bring dead things back to life by 'palingenesis'. Substances like wood could be purified, using the *tria prima*, then 'resuscitated' in their most spiritual form. As Laurence M. Principe points out, this process is analogous to the raising of dead humanity in its perfected form at the moment of Resurrection. As we've seen, empirical observation is not infallible. Even so, it's hard to think what the English diplomat and thinker Sir Kenelm Digby (1603–65) thought he'd seen when he claimed in a London lecture that he'd succeeded in bringing a dead crayfish back to life.

Astraea's Court

John Dee (1527–1608) was held in the highest esteem as Royal Astronomer at the court of Queen Elizabeth I (1533–1603). So seriously were his opinions taken, indeed, that his astrological predictions had been sought in appointing the actual day of her coronation (15 January, 1559). Like the medieval kings, Elizabeth allowed a cult to be constructed around her image and her person, presenting herself as England's 'Virgin Queen'. Big and irascible, her much-married father Henry VIII (1491–1547) had embodied the sulphurous qualities alchemists associated with the sun; Elizabeth could hardly have been more different. Even so, efforts were clearly made to underline the contrast. Her portraits emphasized the pallor that proclaimed her mercurial nature, and her identification with the silver moon; white pearls stand out on her jewel-encrusted costumes.

Her other identification was with the star-white 'Astraea', goddess of justice, innocence and purity. In Greek legend, she was forced to flee the earth by the degeneration of humanity into corruption and lawlessness – Zeus gave her sanctuary as a star (hence the name 'Astraea') in the Virgo constellation. Elizabeth's court poets and painters played with the idea that their queen was Astraea, come back to earth to reinstate the original 'Golden Age' in England.

Das erſt Buch

Dar nach ſoltu haben ofen dar in mā gemeine waſſer

brent mit vier helmen/die in ſand oder in eſchen ſtondt/in mitten zū oberſt ein loch ha
ben/dar in man die kolen werffen iſt/vnnd vnden ein loch dar durch die eſche vnder
dem roſt danen gethon/vnd oben für luſft löcher/dar durch das fūer vnnd hitz vnder
die helm gezogen wūrt. des figur alſo iſt.

Du ſolt ouch haben regiſ-
ter gemacht võ yſen/dar mit zū regiere vil
oder wenig/groß oder clein noch dym bege-
ren/der figur alſo iſt.

Reproduction of a woodcut of alchemical apparatus known as the 'pelican vessel' possibly from Hieronymus Brunschwig's *Liber de arte Distillandi de Compositis*, 1512.

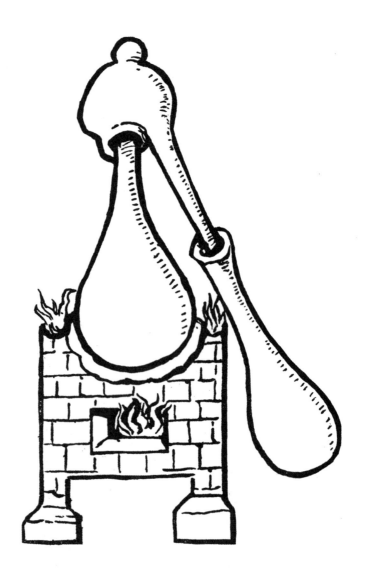

An alembic is an alchemical still consisting of two vessels connected by a tube, used for distilling.

Refining copper using the 'Hungarian' process, 1683.

Astraea takes her flight from earth, as imagined by Salvator Rosa (1665). England's courtiers claimed she'd come back to reign as Queen Elizabeth I.

One characteristic Elizabeth shared with her late father was intellectualism. In girlhood, just for fun, it seems, she'd produced extensive translations from the ancient Latin and Greek authors and more recent books from French and Italian. These were themselves often demanding works of philosophy and history. As Queen she could chat easily with foreign diplomats. In nine different languages, her courtiers claimed. She certainly seems to have been comfortable in French, Italian and Spanish. Where those wouldn't do, she could speak conversationally in Latin.

Hers was a sophisticated court where poets and philosophers were welcome. A man like Dee was always going to fit right in. In his endless curiosity and enterprise, he promoted England's early voyages of exploration (and is said to have first come up with the idea of a 'British Empire').

A Private Project

Even so, by habit secretive, he clearly carved out a more private mental space for himself in which he continued to toil quietly on more esoteric subjects. In the course of these researches, he came up with a 'glyph', a character of his own design to emblematize the interconnectedness of the astronomical, astrological, alchemical and philosophical orders in a single 'monad' – ultimate unity – of existence. It's impossible now to unpack it to any satisfactory extent.

How far it was possible to do so then is debatable: Dee himself wrote a whole book in the attempt, *Monas Hieroglyphica* ('The Hieroglyphic Monad', 1564), but if he succeeded it was at a level of abstruseness few have been able to follow in

the centuries since. Dee's style was purposefully obscure. He had the alchemist's age-old sense that an idea's secrecy was its warranty of truth, and with it the instinct simultaneously to reveal and conceal. Dee's apparently compulsive urge to quibble and pun makes his writing that much more obscure, though he evidently felt wordplay pointed up parallel levels of 'surface' and 'hidden' meaning: you might 'read between the lines' to find a higher truth.

Science and Spirit

Dee's career illustrates the still-ambiguous status of the alchemist. He did much to investigate and popularize non-occult subjects. When Sir Henry Bingley (*c.* 1538–1606) brought out a new translation of Euclid in 1570, Dee wrote a 'Mathematical Preface' which proved profoundly influential in its own right. But he was equally assiduous in pursuing his conversations with the occultist Edward Kelley (1555–97) about *his* purported conversations with the angels.

Not only did he see them, 'scrying' them in a mirror, Kelley maintained, but he had communicated with them via two-way system by which letters marked on tablets were tapped to make up words and longer messages. Alchemical nature abhors transparency, we've seen, so it almost goes without saying that Kelley's angelic contacts tapped out the first third of each message with the words spelled in reverse; in the remaining two-thirds they were given the right way round. Dee had no hesitation in accepting Kelley's claims and became hugely excited at the possibilities they promised to open up. While they didn't offer anything substantial

John Dee's genius is evident, but his work sums up the challenges of alchemy in the age of science. Intriguing and yet utterly perplexing.

Edward Kelley, a magician – 'in the act of invoking the spirit of a deceased person'.
From an illustration published in *The Book of Ceremonial Magic* by Arthur Edward Waite, 1911.

themselves, they were conjurations by which more important angels might be summoned up and persuaded to share the secrets of the Philosopher's Stone.

A Higher Faith

It seems significant that Kelley's conversations were with angels, not more diabolical spirits. Whilst the Faustus story illustrated how easily the alchemist could stray into more diabolical territory, most alchemists were concerned to make it clear that they hadn't left the Christian fold. Dee had been a Catholic under Queen Mary I (1516–58) then converted back to Anglicanism on Elizabeth's accession, but this was only prudent at the time. Besides, it is clear that he was actually passionate in his belief – but, like earlier mystics tended to see faith in spiritual terms that transcended those of specific doctrines. He was open in his hope that he would one day be able to bring the believers of the world together under a single, super-spiritual faith. Indeed, this appears to have been the long-term goal of all his researches and his conversations with the angels.

Certainly, it seems that Kelley knew what he was doing when he conducted his sessions with Dee with a certain amount of religious rigmarole, organizing them as prayerful rituals. It's difficult to avoid a certain cynicism. However high-minded Dee may have been, his companion seems to have been the classic fraud. Kelley finally fell foul of another of his admirers, the Holy Roman Emperor Rudolf II

(1552–1612), who is alleged to have imprisoned him for failing to produce his promised gold. He died in his confinement a few years later.

Running Out of Room?

Kelley's inability to deliver the goods exposed a grubby little fraud, no doubt, but it also illustrates a wider shift that was taking place in the consciousness of the time. As we've seen, Aristotle's empiricism, though right in principle, was limited by the fact that – to put it simply – sometimes what we *think* we see isn't actually what we do. Like the 'fact' that the universe is geocentric – that, in short, the sun, stars and planets revolve around the earth. Copernicus had published his *De revolutionibus orbium coelestium* ('On the Revolutions of the Celestial Spheres') in 1543, suggesting that a 'heliocentric' cosmos was centred on the sun and Johannes Kepler (1571–1630) had carried his work further. Whilst the Danish astronomer Tycho Brahe (1546–1601) would come up with an impressive counterblast for geocentrism, his implicit admission that the cosmos was mechanical and logical (rather than vaguely spiritual) in its workings conceded important ground to the new thinking. His notorious stand against the Inquisition wasn't to take place till 1615, but Galileo (1564–1642) invented his telescope in the 1590s, bringing the planets within reach of real investigation.

It was true, as his Inquisitors said, that Galileo couldn't *prove* that the earth went round the sun – this was the compromise the Church was forced to make with itself for quite some time. But enlightened opinion was evidently on the side of the new thinking, an approach that saw a heliocentric universe as functioning

Robert Boyle represents a generation of Janus-faced scientists who looked forward to a future of scientific reason whilst looking back longingly to the miraculous hopes that alchemy had held out.

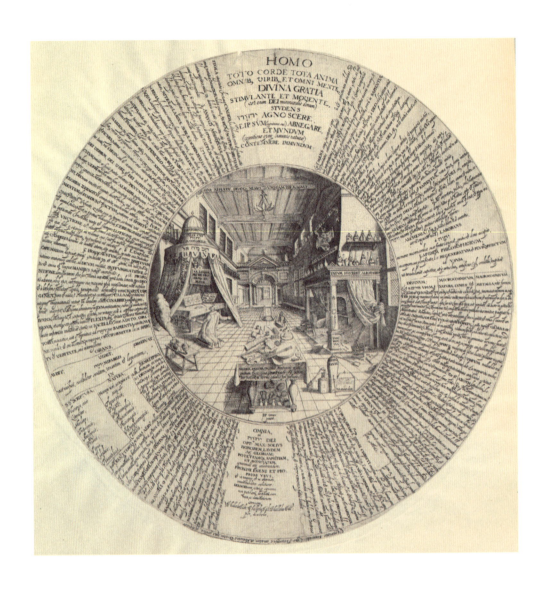

The Alchemist's Laboratory from Heinrich Khunrath, attributed to Peter van der Doort (born Antwerp, active Hamburg ca. 1590–1605).

mechanically. Or mathematically: as Descartes would say, 'With me, everything turns into mathematics'.

Everything obviously didn't in Newton's case. He pursued the prize of the Philosopher's Stone with passionate zeal. But his other findings – in everything from calculus to optics, and of course in mechanics – helped erode the idea that he could ever possibly succeed. Where would a stone with powers like these fit into the universal order he himself was charting with help from the Copernicuses and Keplers?

An Arcane Allure

Many would of course continue to be drawn to the misty esotericism of alchemy. Its obscurantism could be seductive in itself. Newton wasn't the only reputable scientist to hanker after occult insights. The propounder of the famous 'law' on the relationship between volume and pressure in gases, Robert Boyle (1627–91) has widely been acclaimed as the 'Father of Modern Chemistry', but he couldn't help looking wistfully back to the works of weirder forebears. Nor was this just nostalgia. So certain was Boyle that the transmutation of base metal into gold might be achieved in reality in his own day that he lobbied to have Henry IV's 'Act Against Multipliers' repealed, succeeding in 1688.

But the title of his first major book, *The Sceptical Chymist* (1661), was the writing on the wall. A strong advocate for systematic experimentation, he'd taken on board the need Descartes had recognized for doubt. Inside, he was

withering about the inchoateness of the ideas informing the experiments of the Paracelsian alchemists.

The Enlightenment certainly did not bring the study of alchemy to an end. It did, however, reframe it more or less completely. Till now, what passed for 'science' had been squidgy enough in its theoretical underpinnings to accommodate softer, more mystical ideas. The more firmly 'scientific method' became embedded, the less forgiving it could be. Conscious that it too was on shaky scientific ground – and quite possibly on borrowed time – official religion did its best to beef up its rationalistic basis. The idea that a distinguished cleric might moonlight as an alchemist as Roger Bacon or John Dee had simply wasn't going to be imaginable any more.

Coping with Complexity

In time, Newtonian science would itself be challenged for a rigid reductiveness. The rigorous objectivity which scientists had been striving for since the seventeenth century was starting to seem a Philosopher's Stone itself. 'It appears to me,' wrote Albert Einstein (1879–1955), 'that the "real" is an intrinsically empty, meaningless category (pigeon hole), whose monstrous importance lies only in the fact that I can do certain things in it and not certain others.'

Even so, no one has seriously suggested that the complexity quantum physics has opened up affords a space in which alchemy might once more find a scientific function. It seems fated to endure now as no more than a metaphor, for the transformative power of art or love – and the subject of a fascinating history.

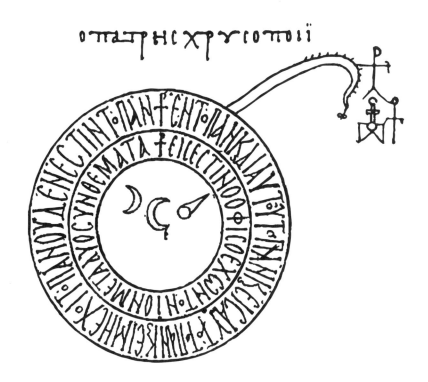

Alchemical illustration from Chrysopoea of Cleopatra.

BIBLIOGRAPHY

Bourke, Stephen, *The Middle East: Cradle of Civilization* (London: Thames & Hudson, 2008).

Eichholz, D.E., 'Aristotle's Theory of the Formation of Metals and Minerals', *Classical Quarterly* Vol. 43, 1949.

Forbes, R.J., 'On the Origins of Alchemy', *Chymia* Vol. 4, 1953.

Forster, E.M., *Alexandria: A History and Guide* (London: Tauris, 2014).

Gilchrist, Cherry, *Alchemy: The Great Work, A History and Evaluation of the Western Hermetic Tradition* (London: Coronet, 2015).

Gosden, Chris, *The History of Magic: From Alchemy to Witchcraft, From the Ice Age to the Present* (London: Penguin, 2021).

Hughes, Jonathan, *The Rise of Alchemy in Fourteenth-Century England: Plantagenet Kings and the Search for the Philosopher's Stone* (London: Continuum, 2012).

Irby-Massie, Georgia L., and Keyser, Paul T., *Greek Science of the Hellenistic Era: A Sourcebook* (London: Routledge, 2001).

Issa, Islam, *Alexandria: The City that Changed the World* (London: Sceptre, 2024).

Jonson, Ben (ed. Gordon Campbell), *The Alchemist and Other Plays* (Oxford: Oxford University Press, 2008).

Keyser, Paul T., 'Alchemy in the Ancient World: From Science to Magic', *Illinois Classical Studies* Vol. 15, 1990.

———, and Irby-Massie, Georgia L., *The Encyclopedia of Ancient Natural Sciences: The Greek Tradition and its Many Heirs* (London: Routledge, 2008).

Makeham, John (ed.), *China: The World's Oldest Living Civilization Revealed* (London: Thames & Hudson, 2008).

Parry, Glyn, *The Arch-Conjuror of England: John Dee* (New Haven, CT: Yale University Press, 2013).

Principe, Lawrence M., *The Secrets of Alchemy* (Chicago: University of Chicago Press, 2013).

Ray, Meredith K., *Daughters of Alchemy: Women and Scientific Culture in Early-Modern Italy* (Cambridge, MA: Harvard University Press, 2015).

Scurlock, Joann, 'Mesopotamian Beginnings for Greek Science?' in Keyser, Paul T., and Scarborough, John (eds), *The Oxford Handbook of Science and Medicine in the Classical World* (Oxford: Oxford University Press, 2018).

Tyldesley, Joyce, *The Penguin Book of Myths and Legends of Ancient Egypt* (London: Penguin, 2011).

Shaw, Ian (ed.), *The Oxford History of Ancient Egypt* (Oxford: Oxford University Press, 2004).

Shaw, Ian, and Nicholson, Paul (eds), *The British Museum Dictionary of Ancient Egypt* (London: British Museum, 2008).

Waddell, Mark A., *Magic, Science, and Religion in Early Modern Europe* (Cambridge: Cambridge University Press, 2021).

PICTURE CREDITS

Alamy: 7 (Science History Images), 9 (Charles Walker Collection), 13 (Chronicle), 22 (World History Archive), 26 (The Natural History Museum), 29 (Art Directors & TRIP), 33 (Science History Images), 37 (Interfoto), 38 (Prisma Archivo), 41 (The Print Collector), 45 (Classic Image), 46 (Artefact), 49 (PhotoStock-Israel), 50 (Azoor Photo), 53 (North Wind Picture Archives), 54 (Album), 57 (Photo 12), 65 (piemags), 66 (Peter Horree), 70 (GL Archive), 74 (The Print Collector), 77 & 78 (CPA Media), 81 (Science History Images), 86 (The Picture Art Collection), 93 (Granger Historical Picture Archive), 94 (World History Archive), 98 (Realy Easy Star), 102 & 105 (CPA Media), 109 (Charles Walker Collection), 110 (Science History Images), 113 (Charles Walker Collection), 117 & 118 (Prisma Archivo), 121 (Science History Images), 130 (Chronicle), 133 (gameover), 136 (Penta Springs), 139 (World History Archive), 140 (Smith Archive), 146 (Album), 149 (World History Archive), 150 (Lebrecht Music & Arts), 153 (Atlaspix)

Creative Commons Attribution-Share alike 4.0 International License: 88 (Rvalette)

Getty Images: 10 (Universal Images Group), 18 (Print Collector), 25 (Ivy Close Images), 34 (Bildagentur), 42 (Culture Club), 55 (Pictures from History), 58 (Bettmann), 69 (Andia/Universal Images Group), 97 (PHAS), 114 (Leemage), 122 (Print Collector), 135 (Photo Josse/Leemage)

Metropolitan Museum of Art, New York: 3, 30, 61, 62, 154

Photos.com: 145

Public Domain: 73, 106

Wellcome Collection: 14, 17, 21, 82, 85, 125, 126, 129, 143, 144